L'CHAIM!

The allure of what would become Greater Miami would eventually have a hold on an entire nation. In 1912 or '13, the Florida East Coast Railway's publicists gave Miami its longtime appellation when they first referred to it as "The Magic City," a pseudonym that has stood the test of time and has come into common usage and the public domain. It would be that mystique, coupled with the sun, sand, charm, lifestyle and business opportunities (not to mention the weather), that would draw innumerable people, including, through the years, those of the Hebrew persuasion, to "come on down" to see, to vacation, to invest and to live. Even today, almost 113 years after the first person of Jewish heritage stood on the shores of Biscayne Bay, Greater Miami remains "The Magic City."

The History of the Jewish Community

L'CHAIM!

of Greater Miami

Seth H. Bramson

Charleston · London
The History Press

Published by The History Press
Charleston, SC 29403
www.historypress.net

Cover design by Marshall Hudson

Unless otherwise credited, all images are courtesy of the author.

First published 2008

Manufactured in the United States

ISBN 978.1.59629.480.6

Library of Congress Cataloging-in-Publication Data

Bramson, Seth, 1944-
L'chaim! : the history of the Jewish community of greater Miami / Seth H. Bramson.
p. cm.
ISBN 978-1-59629-480-6
1. Jews--Florida--Miami--History. 2. Miami (Fla.)--Ethnic relations. I. Title.
F319.M6B738 2008
975.9'381004924--dc22

2008029069

The gratitude of the entire Greater Miami community is owed to the late Ida and Isidor Cohen, Claire Cohen Weintraub, Sydney Weintraub, Murray Cohen and Eddie Cohen. In addition, special thanks are due to the happily very much extant Geri Jane Cohen Riskin, for it was she and other members of her wonderful family, including her cousin, Albert Weintraub, who preserved the Jewish heritage of Greater Miami. It is to Geri, Albert and the Cohen and Weintraub families that this book is lovingly—and gratefully—dedicated.

Contents

Greater Miami Jewish Federation

May 2008

Dear Reader,

If one had to choose a single word to describe Jewish life in South Florida, it would be "community."

No matter where we come from, no matter where we live or work, no matter what our level of religious observance, so many of us feel a powerful connection to our Jewish community.

For 70 years – since the founding of the Greater Miami Jewish Federation in 1938 – our Jewish community has remained united in our commitment to many common ideals: our desire to help Jews in need, both at home and abroad; our devotion to the people of Israel; and our dedication to providing a strong Jewish future for our children and grandchildren. These values are so succinctly summed up in our Mission statement, which is printed at the bottom of our Federation letterhead.

This book provides a glimpse into our Jewish community's fascinating history, and we are delighted to be included in this project. We are prouder still of the role the Greater Miami Jewish Federation has played in shaping the rich heritage that is Jewish Miami.

Sincerely,

Saby Behar
President
2006-2008

Jacob Solomon
Executive Vice President

The Mission of the Greater Miami Jewish Federation is to mobilize human and financial resources to care for those in need, strengthen Jewish life and advance the unity, values and shared purpose of the Jewish people in Miami, in Israel and around the world.

Stanley C. Myers Building • 4200 Biscayne Boulevard, Miami, Florida 33137-3279
Phone: 305-576-4000 • Fax: 305-573-8115 • www.JewishMiami.org

MIAMI JEWISH HOME & HOSPITAL
FOR THE AGED

AT DOUGLAS GARDENS

STEPHEN H. CYPEN
CHAIRMAN OF THE BOARD OF DIRECTORS

February 15, 2008

Dear Friends:

The noted late Justice of the United States Supreme Court Oliver Wendell Holmes, Jr. wrote: "When I want to understand what is happening today or try to decide what will happen tomorrow, I look back."

In January of 1940, a truly visionary woman named Ida Cohen, of blessed memory, invited several friends to her Coral Gables home. She asked their help in organizing a Jewish Home for the elderly to provide a place of safety and dignity for those alone in the winter of their years.

Looking back, the history of the Miami Jewish Home and Hospital (The Home) mirrors the vitality and growth of our community.

Through countless South Floridians who were drawn to her cause, Ida Cohen opened The Home in December of 1945 in a one-story residence with 23 beds, located at 335 Southwest 12th Avenue in the Riverside section of Miami. By January of 1951, the area had grown to the point where The Home needed additional space, and moved to its present 20-acre location in Lemon City.

Today, The Home is one of the nation's largest providers of care, programs and services for the elderly, as well as for people of all ages. The vision of Ida Cohen is one shared and championed for decades by my parents, Hazel and Judge Irving Cypen, with the vital support of The Home's Board members, FOUNDERS, auxilians, staff and volunteers. L'Dor V'Dor, from generation to generation, our organization is privileged to continue this tradition of world-class care.

On behalf of the Miami Jewish Home and Hospital, I am privileged to celebrate the publication of L'Chayim! The History of the Greater Miami Jewish Community. The Home is honored to be included in this meaningful history.

Sincerely,

Stephen H. Cypen
Chairman of the Board

JEWISH MUSEUM OF FLORIDA

ACCREDITED by the AMERICAN ASSOCIATION OF MUSEUMS

April 9, 2008

Dear Reader,

Mazel Tov to Seth Bramson! I am supportive of all vehicles that promote more awareness about Jewish history in Florida. This is what our community needs to enrich the sense of history. Every family has once been immigrants and experienced the acculturation process – this is one group's story – and will be of interest to all.

People other than Catholics have been allowed to live in the Sunshine State only since 1762 when Florida was transferred from Spain to Great Britain. I was astounded 25 years ago to discover that there was no documentation of early Jewish history here and little interest in the subject. This propelled me to travel around the State and gather material evidence of Jewish life in Florida since 1763.

The result was a traveling exhibit that was the genesis of the Jewish Museum of Florida, which opened in 1995 to continue to research, preserve and interpret for the public the Jewish experience in Florida. For Jews, the Museum provides Jewish memories that strengthen Jewish pride and identity to help insure Jewish continuity. For non-Jews, the Museum's exhibitions, public and student programs and statewide outreach help increase tolerance and understanding of different peoples and diminish bigotry through education. This unique South Beach cultural resource is housed in two adjacent historic buildings that were formerly synagogues, and which we connected with a Center Court Café.

I am very proud that our Museum is included as we are a destination for readers of this book who will be inspired to learn and experience more about the history of a group of people who have contributed so much to the development of our community.

Thank you for the opportunity to partner in telling this incredible story.

Marcia Jo Zerivitz
Founding Executive Director & Chief Curator
Jewish Museum of Florida

301 Washington Avenue • Miami Beach, FL • 33139-6965
305-672-5044 • fax 305-672-5933 • www.jewishmuseum.com

Dear Reader,

Beth Torah is delighted to be included in *Seth Bramson's L'Chaim! The History of the Jewish Community of Greater Miami*.

No written history of our Jewish community would be complete without the inclusion of Beth Torah. In fact, one of the largest Jewish communities outside of Israel owes its success in-part to nine men from Monticello, New York. After all, it was these nine men who in 1940 decided to form what was then called the Congregation of Monticello Park.

As the first North-Dade Jewish congregation, Monticello Park was housed originally in a one-room shack on Northeast 163rd Street in North Miami Beach. But, the Conservative congregation quickly outgrew its home.

In 1949, the congregation – now named Beth Torah – dedicated a new, more permanent home in a building erected by its own members.

By its twentieth anniversary and the installation of Rabbi Max Lipschitz in March of 1960, the congregation had again outgrown its home and began planning to build a landmark synagogue on 163rd Street. For its unique and progressive architecture, the building was widely acclaimed and written about.

In 1990, Beth Torah merged with Adath Yeshurun, another long-standing and prominent North Miami Beach congregation.

As one, they moved to a new location – Beth Torah Benny Rok Campus at Northeast 26th Avenue and Ives Dairy Road in Northeast Miami-Dade.

Today, under the religious leadership of Rabbi Edwin Farber and Rabbi Mario Rojzman, Beth Torah is home to a congregation of approximately 600 families. Together, its Scheck Family Religious School, Kettler and Levy Families Youth Connection, Suzy Fischer Early Childhood Academy, and Hochberg Preparatory School comprise more than 700 students.

We join the rest of our community in congratulating the author, publisher and other contributors to this book for their commitment to documenting and keeping alive the unique history of the Jewish people in our community.

L'Chaim!

The Congregants of Beth Torah

The Congregation of Monticello Park

Construction at 163rd Street

Beth Torah Benny Rok Campus

Preface

In approaching the numerous individuals and organizations who so graciously contributed to this book, the results were, for the most part, strongly positive. In several cases people who did not have material were kind enough to refer me to others who did. Occasionally, somebody would "come out of the woodwork," telling me that they had heard about the book and wanted to contribute, and those calls were always welcome. In most cases, those whom I approached were gracious, receptive and helpful to the "nth" degree. Regretfully, however, a very small minority was disinterested. While they shall remain nameless, the reader may be assured that for them, more is the pity.

One other quite valid point should also be noted. This writer's history of Miami Beach was the first-ever history of that great city written by somebody who grew up on, lived on, went to school on and worked on Miami Beach, and one cannot write about Miami Beach (well, legally, of course, one can, although that writing will be without the heart, feeling and understanding that it takes to write about such an incredible and unique place) unless one has fulfilled the four qualifications noted immediately above. So it is with a book on Jewish institutions or Jewish people.

A book written by a *goy* that deals intimately with Jewish topics, people or institutions is and will be, simply put, lacking, and it is a *shanda* for the neighbors of a Jewish organization not to have its history commemorated by a member of the tribe, for it cannot and will not have the same level or depth of feeling and understanding as a book on the subject written by a *landsman.* As with writing about Miami Beach, one cannot write about Jewish institutions or the Jewish community unless he or she is part of—and *knows*—that community.

The other reason for this preface is to advise the reader that this book is not and was not meant to be a compendium of every Jewish person or family who has ever lived in Greater Miami, and it is not meant to enumerate every event, happenstance or organization, nor is it a list of every temple or synagogue that ever existed in Miami-Dade County. Rather, it is meant to tell a story, and that incredible story is of a community that began by chance with the arrival of one person in a near-wilderness frontier region in February of 1896. With his observing it, participating in it and commenting on its fads and foibles through the fifty-five years until his death in 1951, it has become one of the most active, buoyant, responsive and vibrant Jewish communities in America, if not the world.

However, and in response to those who might have unintentionally been slighted, or who have a story to tell or who, perhaps, should have been included, my regrets are wholehearted and fulsome, and I assure the reader that only a very few people were either ignored or left out intentionally. I ask that readers recognize that the number of pages was limited, the number of photographs was constrained by space and the amount of information emanating from the more than 112 years of the existence of Greater Miami's Jewish community borders on infinite.

Those who do have more to tell or add are asked to contact the author in Miami and every effort will be made to include those people and their stories in the next edition.

Until then, "to life...to life...l'chaim!" May you learn from—and greatly enjoy—this book!

Acknowledgements

The list of those who must be thanked is, happily, long! Rabbi Gary Glickstein and Alice Miller, executive director of Temple Beth Sholom, welcomed me warmly and opened the temple's historic files for me; Belle Lehrman graciously allowed me to go through the late Rabbi Lehrman's photos and memorabilia; Alexa Weiss Rossy provided innumerable images and memorabilia from her fabled family's past; Dr. Arlene Arvan Amarant replied to every question about her equally fabled family history; Marcia Zerivitz, executive director of the Jewish Museum of Florida, unhesitatingly stepped forward to assist; Stephen Cypen, chairman of the board of the Miami Jewish Home and Hospital, was highly supportive; Bonnie Reiter Lehrer and Judy Gilbert Gould at Federation were marvelous in putting together material for me and I am especially grateful to all of them for their help and assistance.

My friends and fellow Miami memorabilia collectors Phil Spool and Dr. Abe Lavender graciously provided the photos of Temple Beth Tov Ahavat Shalom, and Ella Galvan so kindly loaned the very rare photographs and yearbook from Temple Tifereth Jacob in Hialeah. Steve Rice, of Beth Torah Congregation, bent over backward to be of help.

Special note must be made of the kindness extended to me by Sandie Morrison, publisher and president of *The Real Florida Jewish Directory*, who unhesitatingly gave me permission to utilize the list of Miami-Dade synagogues, temples and chabads that are in that book.

Stu Graver; June and Stu Jacobs; Julian Newbauer of Kirk Jewelers; June Levy Newbauer; Al and Hannah (Diamond) Lipton; Ann Broad Bussel; Morris Broad; Ileene and Chuck Wallace; my dear Myra Farr and equally dear Fran Gardner; Norma and Michael Orovitz; Felicia Deutch; Professor Judy Malschick; Barbara and Barry Sugerman; Karen Lytton Levin; Judges Larry Schwartz, Leon Firtel and federal district Judge Alan S. Gold; Chief Judge of the Eleventh Judicial District Joseph Farina; Alicia and Alan Sirkin; Ann Martin Schneider; Janet Cowan and Michael Cowan; Mickey and Sherman Tobin; Sidell Levine; Yetta Brodie; Kathy Friedman; Reggie Perlmutter Goldstein; Shelley Miller; Sheldon Miller (two different Millers!); Dorothy and Dr. Maurice Serotta; Marlene Reiss; Gloria Pallot; Howard Katzen; Richard Schulman;

Barbara Seitlin Gillman; Dr. Carole (Spitzer) and Dr. Isadore Newman; Josh Fuller and his family; Bookie and David Rogers; Gail and Mario Talucci; Stephanie and Bobby Hauser; Arlene Bercun; Quentin Sandler and his beautiful daughter, Gail Sandler Reiss; Delsie Lipton; Ricky Neross; Selma and Ben Grenald; Henry Mangels; Jim Gordon; Temple Beth Am; the Rabbi Alexander S. Gross Hebrew Academy; Marilyn and Teddy Blake; the descendants of Pepi and Meinhardt Bergida (including Dr. Pepi Granat, Mickey Tobin, Judge David Tobin and Dr. Arlene Arvan Amarant); Marcia Kanner; Joyce Cohen and Danny Weintraub; Margie and Ron Alter; Lenore Gaynor; Jane and Jerry Goodman; retired assistant director of Miami-Dade Police Irving Heller; Biscayne Park Chief of Police Mitchell Glansberg; Patsy and Alan Glaser; Yaffa Dermer; photographers Al Barg and Jeff Weisberg; Rosalind (Roz) Merritt; Audrey Sweet; Drs. Alam and Bill Berke; Ron Silvers; Dr. Susannah Worth; and Miami historian Sara B. Leviten all contributed photos and/or information that were and have been invaluable in researching and preparing this book. To all of them, "Great thanks, sir!"

Through a chance meeting I was, thanks to my beloved brother, Bennett Bramson, introduced to Adam Rogers, who did such a marvelous job scanning the images for this book, and I thank Adam sincerely for his great and careful work.

Finally, words are never enough to thank the woman who has put up with all of this *mischigass* and *tummeling* for the three years I chased her before she finally caught me and the thirty-two years of marriage that she has managed to get through, mostly with that beautiful smile of hers. She is special beyond words and my gratitude—and love—for her are boundless and endless. It is only too bad that all I can say is, "Thank you, Myrna."

INTRODUCTION

This is a story of such magnitude, such depth, such power and such historic proportions that, were it not real and true, it could be mistaken for a fantasy. Be assured that it is anything but that!

With the arrival of one Isidor Cohen in a not yet formally named place on the shores of Biscayne Bay in February of 1896, the story and history of the Jewish community of what would someday become Greater Miami would begin. That inauspicious beginning has led, though the past more than 112 years, to one of the most recognized, important, dedicated and influential groups of Jewish individuals and families in America. It is sometimes difficult to understand why Jewish people might have wanted to come to the southeastern tip of Florida in 1896 and for several years thereafter unless one recognizes that the Jewish settlers were just like everyone else who came here: adventuresome pioneers who believed that they could, in a place that was still near-wilderness until the early years of the twentieth century, build their homes, open their businesses and make their fortunes on the banks of the Miami River. In short, they were the pioneers, and it is from them—particularly Ida and Isidor Cohen—that the story and history of the Jewish community emanates.

The Jewish people who came to southeast Florida settled, initially, in what would become downtown Miami, their homes generally within walking distance of their businesses. But as the area grew, the new arrivals settled farther away, and the history of Greater Miami is replete with Jewish citizens and individuals having an influence in and on Miami, Miami Beach, Coral Gables, southwest and northeast Dade County and the beachfront communities north of Miami Beach. Even Hialeah had a temple and a not inconsequential Jewish presence.

What began as "a few drops" turned into a trickle and then a virtual flood as, following World War II, thousands of people, no few Jews among them, came back after the war to where they had done their training, to what they believed to be nothing short of paradise: a sun-drenched, frost, snow and blizzard–free near-nirvana, where the opportunities for one to make a living were unending. Although there were disturbing instances—no few of them on Miami Beach—of restrictions against Jewish people staying in certain hotels, the leadership of the Jewish community, which was by then an integral part of the fabric of society of the entire area, eventually prevailed upon both private interests and government and the restrictions faded into history, although the last of them did survive in Bal Harbour until the mid-1970s.

The Jewish interest in and influence on education was apparent in the founding of the University of Miami, and the Jewish people have become great and major contributors to the various educational institutions including Barry University, Miami-Dade College, Florida International University and the aforementioned U of Miami.

Their unending interest in the arts and culture has led them to either found or strongly support the Museum of Science, the Jewish Museum of Florida, the various orchestras, the Opera Guild of Greater Miami, the Ballet, the Bass Museum of Art on Miami Beach, the Museum of Contemporary Art in North Miami, the Wolfsonian—FIU and the Miami Design Preservation League—founded by the late, great Barbara Capitman—which, almost single-handedly and against endless obstacles won the support of the city, state and federal governments in having a large section of today's "SoBe" (once known as South Beach) declared a national historic district. Additionally, many other institutions, including the various county and city libraries, parks and recreational venues, have received almost unlimited support from Jewish individuals, families and organizations.

The dedication of primarily Jewish donors is what has brought about the success of many healthcare institutions in Greater Miami, not the least of them being the Miami Jewish Home and Hospital for the Aged at Douglas Gardens and Mount Sinai Hospital on Miami Beach.

Suffice to say, as in most of the rest of the country, if the Jewish people had not been so active, involved and prominent in the areas of business, education, the arts and sciences and the professions, the region would have been far poorer in many ways besides financially. The richness of the Jewish traditions of education, learning and philanthropy have enriched Greater Miami more than words can express.

It is hoped that the reader will, within these pages, garner a sense and grasp a feeling of the immensity of the Jewish contributions to South Florida, recognizing that the people—named and unnamed, rich or poor, captains of industry or hourly or salaried employees—all have helped to weave the incredible mosaic that is and has been a great and major part of the life, times and events of one of the most unique and unusual places on earth. Simply put, this book is a tribute to the Jewish community of South Florida and all who have had a part in building it.

Chapter One

Ida and Isidor Cohen

The story and history of Miami's Jewish community must, perforce, begin with one person: Isidor Cohen. Cohen was born in Russia in 1870 and came to the United States with his parents in 1883, becoming a naturalized citizen in Savannah, Georgia, in 1891. In 1893 he moved to Florida, but not, as the *Miami Herald* wrote, to Miami. In fact, he would not move to Miami until February of 1896.

Actually, Isidor Cohen had been preceded by at least one other Jewish fellow, who, finding the heat, humidity, mosquitoes, undergrowth and generally wild conditions not to his liking, departed within a few weeks of his arrival. Interestingly, Ida's first husband, Jacob Schneidman, came to Miami close to or at nearly the same time as Cohen did. Jacob, however, died from cancer on September 1, 1903.

Schneidman and his brother, Harry, operated a furniture store at 1306 Avenue D (on today's Miami Avenue, a bit more than a block past what is now Southwest First Street, on the west side of the street), while Harry lived at 425 Tenth Street, which is today's Northeast and Northwest Second Street.

Cohen arrived on February 6, 1896, to a place that was bustling in preparation for the soon-to-arrive Florida East Coast Railway. He relates that he traveled on the FEC from West Palm Beach to the railroad's then terminal at Fort Lauderdale, thence via a small steamboat to Lemon City, a part of today's city of Miami now known as "Little Haiti."

Upon reaching the Miami River, several miles south of Lemon City, Cohen related, in his wonderful 1925 self-published tome, "Historical Sketches and Sidelights of Miami, Florida," that he had an interview with the fabled Julia Tuttle, the "mother of Miami," regarding renting property from her on the north side of the Miami River. The results were disappointing.

Showing his marvelous sense of humor, Cohen relates that he was told that he had to wait until the land was cleared and the streets were laid out. He explained to Mrs. Tuttle that he was, due to his "destitute condition," unable to wait, whereupon she suggested that he take a job clearing land. Turning to Mrs. Tuttle, he wrote that he tried to impress "this naïve lady" that "the last labor of that character my race had performed was in the land of Egypt, and that it would be a violation of my religious convictions to resume that condition of servitude!"

Following various machinations in arranging to bring his goods into Miami, finding a suitable location upon which to open a store and confirming his housing arrangements, Cohen set out to acquaint himself with the vagaries of the area, its geographic nuances and the fads and foibles of the people, tasks which history has proven he was eminently successful at.

On April 22, 1896, Cohen was among the approximately three hundred people who watched the first FEC passenger train arrive. The very first train, a work and supply unit, had arrived one week earlier. Cohen relates that he got to meet Henry Flagler as well as Flagler's lieutenants James E. Ingraham, Joseph R. Parrott and R.T. Goff, the FEC's superintendent; these men have since become famous in Florida history.

Although references in the aforementioned *Miami Herald* state that Mr. Cohen "used to say that until 1909 he was one of two Jewish residents of Miami," the facts belie that comment. His 1925 book notes that among the early (1897) residents were Louis Woolf the tailor, J.M. Frank (who died in the 1905 fire that destroyed much of what was then downtown and led to the imposition of building codes calling for brick buildings) and David Singer, Sam Singer and Jacob Schneidman, who Cohen referred to as "merchants." Further, Cohen noted that when the 1896 fire struck, all but four of the sixteen retail merchants were of the Jewish faith.

On December 25, 1896, fire struck the young city, ravaging the businesses that were situated on or adjacent to Twelfth Street (today's Flagler Street) and Avenue D (today's Miami Avenue). Following that fire, Cohen and Schneidman entered into a partnership so that each was part owner of the other's business. Following Schneidman's 1903 passing, Cohen purchased Schneidman's half of the business and brought his (Cohen's) own brother Harry to Miami to help him operate it.

In August of 1904, Isidor went north, ostensibly on a buying trip. But during that trip he married the former Ida Herkowitz (some sources show it spelled as Herskowitz) Schneidman, and adopted her son, Murray, whose surname became Cohen. On June 1, 1905, daughter Claire was born and in 1908 son Edward (Eddie) was born. As is still customary with the *Miami Herald*, the paper erroneously reported, upon Eddie's death on June 26, 1967, that he was sixty-four and that he was the first Jewish child born in Miami, completely ignoring the fact that Eddie was fifty-nine when he died, that Claire was three years older than Eddie and that *she* was actually the first Jewish child born in Miami!

In 1900, recognizing the need for a formal merchants' group, Isidor Cohen was at the forefront of organizing the Miami Board of Trade. In 1902 the Miami Merchants Association was holding meetings, and in 1903 Cohen became president with John Burdine as the group's secretary. Cohen, by 1907, also served as treasurer of the Board of Trade. In 1913, the two groups merged to form the Miami Chamber of Commerce, with Isidor Cohen its first secretary.

Ida, not to be outdone, was a member of the Women's Club (for many years their only Jewish member) and founded several organizations locally. Her greatest achievement and accomplishment, however, would be spearheading the formation of the Miami Jewish Home and Hospital for the Aged in 1940. Today located at Douglas Gardens (the site of the home and gardens of longtime Miami businessman E.B. Douglas), the home is the highest-rated facility of its type in the South.

The superlatives of the Cohen family are endless, and daughter Claire would continue the tradition and uphold the legacy, founding the Miami Museum of Science and becoming its first president. In 1928, Claire graduated in the University of Miami's first class. Some years later she would be presented with an honorary doctorate from that now world-class institution in recognition of her achievements and accomplishments in the community as well as her contributions to the school.

In October of 1928, following graduation, she married Philadelphian Sydney Weintraub and their marriage, like her parents' union, lasted a lifetime until Claire's untimely death from a stroke (*Miami Daily News*) or from "a brain infection" (the *Miami Herald*), the *News*'s statement more likely correct. Ironically, husband Sydney was in the same hospital recovering from a serious illness when Claire died there. Sydney Weintraub became one of Miami's most prominent attorneys and the Weintraubs' son, Albert, became a partner in a law firm headlined by recently retired chief federal district bankruptcy judge A. Jay Cristol.

Eddie Cohen spent many years as a sports columnist for the *Miami News* while Murray worked for Florida Power & Light (FP&L) Company, likely brought in by the late and revered "Hy" Hyman, who was probably FP&L's first Jewish employee. While Eddie did not have children, he was adored by his nieces and nephews, including Geri Jane Cohen Riskin, who was Murray's daughter and Ida and Isidor's granddaughter.

Suffice to say, the Cohen–Weintraub–Riskin story and legacy would require a large book. The work that they have done on behalf of all Miamians, not just the members of the Jewish community, is the stuff of legend and the Cohen family and its descendants deserve to be honored (if not revered) for as long as there is and will be a Miami.

Photographed with her first-grade class at Miami Central School, six-year-old Claire Cohen is seated fourth from right in the first row. This photograph was most likely taken in 1911.

A 1920 studio portrait shows, from left, Claire, Eddie, Ida and Murray, with the patriarch, Isidor, seated in front of them.

Photographs such as this are both priceless and irreplaceable, for they show the people, the attire of the times, the event and the venue. Claire and Sydney were married on Tuesday evening, October 16, 1928, at Temple Beth David. Prior to the wedding Claire, standing in the exact center, was shown at the Cohen home with her bridesmaids, ring bearer and flower children. It must have been a gala event!

Likely taken in front of their Miami Beach home, Sydney, at left, has Albert on his knee while Claire smiles warmly and lovingly.

Ida, Albert's pup and Albert posed for this photo in either the Cohen or the Weintraub home. While, happily for us, the photo exists, nobody today remembers in which house the view was made.

A joyous day, the proud family poses together for Albert and Sara Lee's nuptials. From left are Sydney's mother, Sydney, Sara Lee, Albert, Claire and Ida.

Claire was a major force in Miami's social, philanthropic and art communities. In addition, she was a tireless volunteer and is shown here at right on the platform of a WQAM radio World War II war bonds fundraiser, likely in downtown Miami. The other two participants are not known to us today.

Miami, Fla. June 2nd, '37

Baron DeHirsh Meyer
First Trust Bdg.
Miami, Fla.

Congratulations on your victory Stop Your brilliant success proves that a well-behaved and discreet Jew will not fail to secure the support of non-Jews Stop It is the non-Jewish vote that placed you close to the leading candidate Stop The vote of your coreligionists was badly split up. The result of the election is not only a personal testimonial to you but a rebuke to anti-Semites and to envious coreligionists.

Isidor Cohen

MEYER, DAVIS & WEISS
ATTORNEYS AT LAW
FIRST TRUST AND SAVINGS BANK BUILDING
MIAMI, FLORIDA

BARON DE HIRSCH MEYER
DARREY A. DAVIS
MILTON WEISS

June 17, 1937

Mr. Isidor Cohen,
Safe Deposit Bldg.,
Miami, Fla.

Dear Mr. Cohen:

I wish to thank you for your very thoughtful telegram upon my re-election to the City Council.

It is true, the vote that I received was due in a large part to the non-jewish support. Unfortunately, I did not receive as much support from the jews as I should have; but it is, as you say, the jews are a peculiar people, and I suppose we must recognize their weaknesses and peculiarities. In any event it is now all over, and I hope that I may be able to be of service to both jews and non-jews as well.

Cordially yours,

Baron De Hirsch Meyer

This page: One of Greater Miami's most renowned philanthropists was Baron deHirsch Meyer, the first Jewish person elected to Miami Beach City Council. When Meyer won his 1937 bid for reelection, Isidor sent him the telegram shown here, which remarked upon the deportment of Jews running for office and noted that the election results were not only "a testimonial to you but a rebuke to anti-Semites and envious co-religionists." DeHirsch Meyer's response was classic, he being his usual gracious self while generous to those who may have been his detractors.

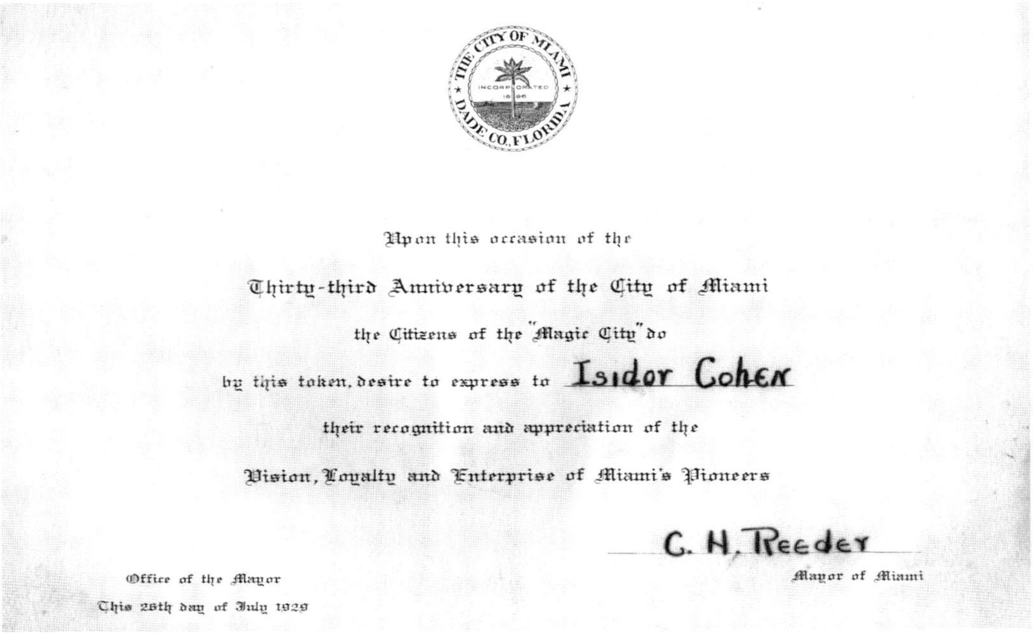

The City of Miami · Dade Co. Florida · Incorporated 1896

Upon this occasion of the

Thirty-third Anniversary of the City of Miami

the Citizens of the "Magic City" do

by this token, desire to express to Isidor Cohen

their recognition and appreciation of the

Vision, Loyalty and Enterprise of Miami's Pioneers

C. H. Reeder
Mayor of Miami

Office of the Mayor
This 28th day of July 1929

Above: On July 28, 1929, the thirty-third anniversary of Miami's founding, Isidor was honored with a Certificate of Appreciation for his vision, loyalty and enterprise as one of Miami's pioneers. The certificate was duly inscribed by Mayor C.H. Reeder.

Right: The joyfulness of being a proud grandfather is obvious and evident on Isidor's face, as he sits proudly with grandson Albert.

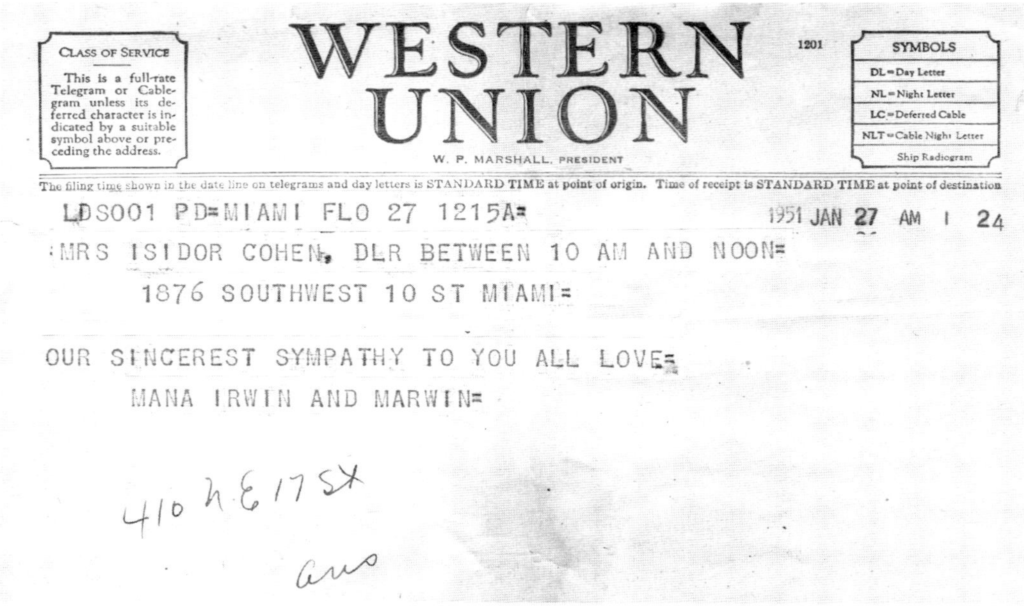

CLASS OF SERVICE

This is a full-rate Telegram or Cablegram unless its deferred character is indicated by a suitable symbol above or preceding the address.

WESTERN UNION

W. P. MARSHALL, PRESIDENT

1201

SYMBOLS

DL=Day Letter

NL=Night Letter

LC=Deferred Cable

NLT=Cable Night Letter

Ship Radiogram

The filing time shown in the date line on telegrams and day letters is STANDARD TIME at point of origin. Time of receipt is STANDARD TIME at point of destination

LDS001 PD=MIAMI FLO 27 1215A= 1951 JAN 27 AM 1 24

:MRS ISIDOR COHEN, DLR BETWEEN 10 AM AND NOON=

1876 SOUTHWEST 10 ST MIAMI=

OUR SINCEREST SYMPATHY TO YOU ALL LOVE=

MANA IRWIN AND MARWIN=

410 N E 17 St

ans

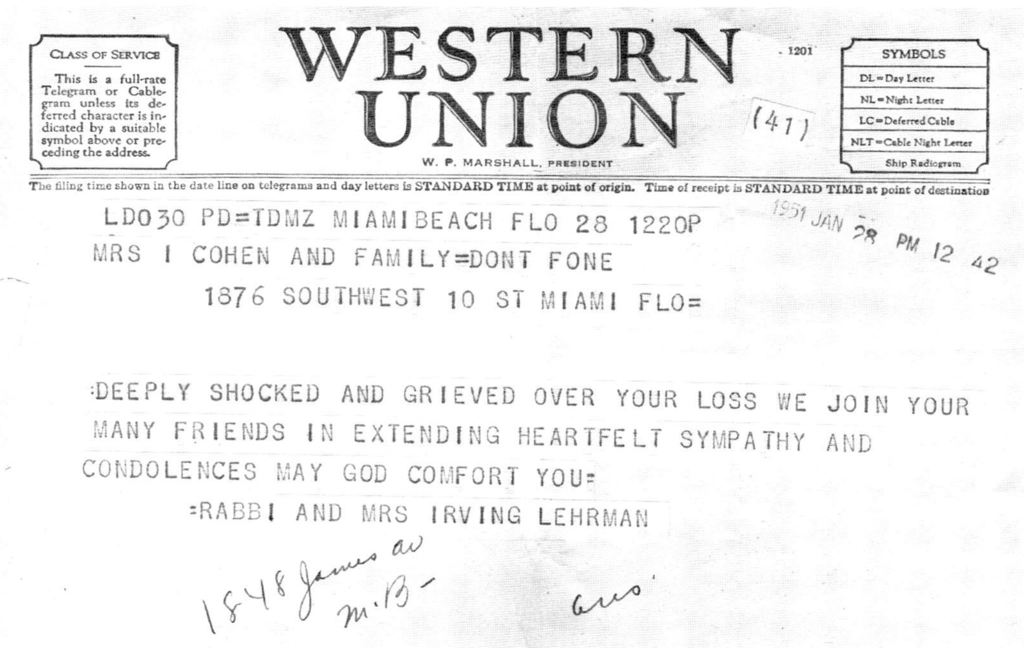

CLASS OF SERVICE

This is a full-rate Telegram or Cablegram unless its deferred character is indicated by a suitable symbol above or preceding the address.

WESTERN UNION

W. P. MARSHALL, PRESIDENT

1201

(41)

SYMBOLS

DL=Day Letter

NL=Night Letter

LC=Deferred Cable

NLT=Cable Night Letter

Ship Radiogram

The filing time shown in the date line on telegrams and day letters is STANDARD TIME at point of origin. Time of receipt is STANDARD TIME at point of destination

LD030 PD=TDMZ MIAMIBEACH FLO 28 1220P 1951 JAN 28 PM 12 42

MRS I COHEN AND FAMILY=DONT FONE

1876 SOUTHWEST 10 ST MIAMI FLO=

:DEEPLY SHOCKED AND GRIEVED OVER YOUR LOSS WE JOIN YOUR MANY FRIENDS IN EXTENDING HEARTFELT SYMPATHY AND CONDOLENCES MAY GOD COMFORT YOU=

=RABBI AND MRS IRVING LEHRMAN

1848 James av M.B.

ans

This page: Following Isidor's death on Thursday night, January 25, 1951, the entire area was in mourning. One of Miami's greatest pioneers and founders was gone, and his arrival in February of 1896 had been an event almost as momentous as the arrival of the FEC Railway two months later, although very few realized it at the time. Innumerable tributes poured into the Cohen home, including the telegrams shown here from two of Miami's most prominent families: the great music impresario Mana Zuca, her husband Irwin Cassel and their son, Marwin; and Rabbi Irving and Belle Lehrman, he the longtime spiritual head of Temple Emanu-el on Miami Beach.

They were a family of contributors: to the arts, to education, to music, to science, to almost any worthy cause, and to the end of each of their days they remained active in the larger Miami community, revered by all who knew them, loved by so many whose lives they touched. Claire doted on her mother and was with her on many of the occasions during which Ida was honored. This photo was likely taken at one of the events commemorating Ida's work in founding the Miami Jewish Home and Hospital.

Chapter Two

The Early Years

In retrospect, looking back over more than a century of its incredible existence, "the early years" of Miami and its Jewish community should, from the perspective of the first decade of the twenty-first century, include the years from the 1896 arrival of Isidor Cohen to and through the separation from Temple Beth David of a group of Reform Jews, which resulted in the founding of Temple Israel in 1922, and through the 1929 opening of Temple Beth Jacob on Miami Beach, that city's first synagogue. However, several incidents and occurrences should and will be noted, even though they are several years beyond the previously mentioned 1929 date.

The purpose of this book is not to provide a detailed history of the events and actions that led to certain individuals and their differing beliefs engendering a schism within Beth David, but it should be noted that the issue was, in its simplest terms, the struggle for control of the then-only temple in Miami between the Reform group and the Conservative group. That struggle would lead to Temple Israel's birth.

Miami was devastated by the fires of 1896, 1899 and 1905, as well as a series of yellow fever epidemics, and it was following the 1905 fire that the ordinance was passed requiring the downtown buildings to be of brick construction. After the passage of that requirement, growth could—and did—begin. In 1910, Mr. Cohen estimated that the city had five Jewish merchants as well as an additional eight or ten adult males in "other occupations," possibly professional trades but likely not laborers. Florida's 1915 census noted that there were 15,437 residents in Miami, while the city directory of 1923 showed a population of 51,000, although that may have included Miami Beach.

Although the Miami Jews had purchased a cemetery in 1912, one of the reasons for the slow growth of the Jewish population, at least according to Cohen, was that there were no "brick and mortar" institutions in which Jews could enjoy communal life: no temples, no Jewish community centers (JCCs) and no gathering places for Jewish youth (YMHAs).

Meanwhile, Joe Weiss started cooking at Smith's Casino on Ocean Beach (later Miami Beach) in 1913. Five years later, following a disagreement with the casino's owners, Joe opened a seafood restaurant on the farthest south street of what by then was Miami

Beach. Joe's Restaurant, at 227 Biscayne Street, would eventually become Joe's Stone Crabs and the rest, of course, is history.

The Ungar family—including Bertha (later Bertha Abess), who was three at the time—which was later well known for its automobile dealership, arrived in Miami in 1918. Daughter Marcella (later Marcella Werblow) was born in 1920. The Kanner family, which had started visiting, according to Marcia Kanner, in late 1896, opened a retail business but due to the heat, mosquitoes and other discomforts did not stay long. However, they did move to Miami permanently in 1925, Aaron Kanner becoming one of the city's most prominent attorneys.

In 1922, Morris Zion founded the Jewish Welfare Board, today known as Jewish Family and Children's Services. That same year, the group that supported Reform Judaism left Temple Beth David to found Temple Israel. Beth David, which had been formed and organized as a Conservative temple, had a fairly large number of Orthodox adherents who eventually left the temple and formed Miami Orthodox Congregation in 1931. That group was later known as Miami Hebrew Congregation and finally as Temple Beth El.

Interestingly, another Weiss family is prominent in Miami Beach's history: the family of Milton and Cecile (Ceecee) Alexander Weiss. Milton's mother, Rose, came to Miami Beach in 1919 and took up residence at the Royal Apartments at 221 Collins Avenue. Milton was then four years old. (Milton's name, incidentally, appears on the letterhead on page twenty-six, which was sent by Baron deHirsch Meyer to Isidor Cohen in 1937.) Rose's daughter, Malvina (Weiss) Liebman, became head of elementary education in Dade County, remaining in that position for many years. Rose's son, Dr. Eugene Weiss, with his office on Lincoln Road, was a highly respected podiatrist and civic activist.

In 1932, the Alexander family arrived and Ceecee graduated from Ida M. Fisher High School in 1934, in the next to last class prior to the school's name being changed to Miami Beach High School.

Along with those families the Granat family must also be noted. Velma (also known as Mully or Nema by her numerous granddaughters, grandsons, nieces and nephews) arrived in Miami and came to Miami Beach, according to granddaughter Dr. Pepi Granat, in 1919. She and her husband David built the David (first known as the St. David because, according to Velma, David was "a saint!") Court Hotel at 56 Washington Avenue. The first Jewish religious services on Miami Beach were held on the third floor of that building, prior to the construction and completion of Temple Beth Jacob at 311 Washington Avenue. Several years later, the congregation purchased the property immediately south at 301 Washington Avenue, the former temple later becoming the Jewish Museum of Florida.

The Granats began bringing relatives down from New York and many of Greater Miami's most prominent families—including the Bergida, Granat, Arvan, Quittner, Tobin, Landesman, Schwarz, Schwartz and Klein families, all of whom are related—spring from Pepi and Meinhardt Bergida, who were Velma's parents. They are both buried in Woodlawn Cemetery in Miami. Like both Weiss families and so many others, the contributions of the pioneers cannot be either overlooked or forgotten.

The importance of the Jewish people in the area was spreading and for a short time one Edward E. "Doc" Dammers worked as the sales manager for Miami Beach's founder, Carl Fisher. Dammers left Fisher (the reason, though never publicly stated, may have been the anti-Semitic bent of Fisher and several of the other builders of the beach, including Thomas Pancoast) and within a short time turned up in Coral Gables, where, working for George Merrick, the builder of "the City Beautiful," he established a reputation as a super-salesman, one day taking in something close to $2 million in land sales. Dammers became the first mayor of Coral Gables. But what few people were aware of, then or now, was that "Doc" was Jewish. I believe that, unlike in certain other parts of the county including Bal Harbour, Miami Beach and Miami Shores, there were no deed restrictions or covenants on land sales in Coral Gables excluding persons of "Semitic origin" from buying property. Further, the first chief of police in the Gables was M.P. "Pop" Lehman, and though it cannot be signed in blood as absolute fact, it is likely that "Pop" was brought in by Dammers and was also of the Jewish faith.

The influx of Jews into the area was increasing yearly and the separation of what would become Temple Israel from Beth David, along with the opening of the first temple on Miami Beach, correctly indicates that the Jewish population was reaching a point from which growth would go from arithmetical to close to exponential. The new era, however, would bring a new set of problems and issues, and one of the unhappiest—if not the unkindest—of them would be the refusal of no few hoteliers and apartment house owners to rent hotel rooms or lease apartments to those known to be of the Jewish faith.

Unquestionably and without dispute, Julia Tuttle was "the mother of Miami." Through her dogged persistence and actions following the great freezes of December of 1894 and January and February of 1895, the legendary Henry M. Flagler—the eventual recipient of half of her holdings north of the Miami River and half of the holdings of Mary and William Brickell south of the river—extended the Florida East Coast Railway to the shores of Biscayne Bay and built the Royal Palm Hotel, for thirty years the center of Miami's social and business life, on the banks of the Miami River.

Standing at the southwest corner of Avenue D and Twelfth Street (Miami Avenue and Flagler Street), we are looking northeast on Twelfth Street at the Frank T. Budge Hardware and Furniture store prominent across the street. Budge and his brother are mentioned several times in Cohen's 1925 tome and it is likely that Isidor and Ida purchased much—if not most—of their home and business furnishings from Budge, who was a fellow pioneer and member of several groups in which Isidor was active.

One of the Miami Grocery Company's delivery vehicles, with a Schlitz sign on either side painted by T.M. Bryant. *Courtesy Henry Mangels.*

It was a bright, sunny day in March in the early 1920s, and we are looking west on just renamed Flagler Street. Miami College of Dance and Dr. Sheehan's dentist's office are in the building just beyond the cafeteria. Just past them is the Hotel McCrory, with Western Union farther up the street. On the left is Sewell's, which brothers John and Everest claimed as "Miami's first store." Farther west are Rector's Café and Burdine's, which called itself "The Heart of Miami."

Coral Gables' Biltmore Hotel, one of America's most magnificent hostelries, was built by George Merrick and John McEntee Bowman. Unlike a good few Miami Beach hotels, hotels in "the Gables" were not known to be restricted.

In 1923, the Miami Chamber of Commerce published this beautiful "Miami by the Sea" booklet, the visible side featuring "cheesecake," the beautiful girl in the bathing suit posing on the beach on Miami Beach. The other side is a view of a golfer teeing off at the FEC Hotel Company–owned golf course, which is now the site of Miami-Dade's government center and hospitals complex.

The streetcar system in Greater Miami was expanding rapidly and eventually Miami, Miami Beach and Coral Gables would each have their own lines. Shown here, big double truck Birney trolley 301 sits on either Alton Road or Washington Avenue prior to heading back across the County (now MacArthur) Causeway to Miami.

The first religious ceremonies for Jewish families on Miami Beach were conducted on the top floor of the David Court Hotel at 56 Washington Avenue beginning in 1925. For several years, the hotel, owned by the Granat family, served as the unofficial meeting place of and for the Jewish community. *Courtesy Judge David Tobin.*

Bessie and Isadore Gaynor moved to Miami with son Milton in 1924. Following the 1926 hurricane, they moved across the bay to Miami Beach, and in 1930 Milton became one of the first bar mitzvahs in the original building of the newly opened Temple Beth Jacob. *Courtesy Lenore Gaynor.*

Chapter Three

More Than Forty Years of Restricted Clientele

As noted previously it is possible, if not likely, that Doc Dammers left the employ of Carl Fisher and Thomas Pancoast due to their less than favorable feelings regarding Jewish clientele. Further, unless Fisher determined that one was "acceptable," a person of the Jewish faith was not necessarily welcome at his hotels (the Lincoln, Nautilus, King Cole and Flamingo), as noted in the Lincoln Hotel brochure shown in this chapter.

The stories abound regarding whether Jews could purchase property north of Fifth Street on Miami Beach prior to 1920, and Dr. Abe Lavender, founder and president of the Miami Beach Historical Association, had long been seeking documentation as to the validity of those tales. Fortunately, my collection provides proof that at least some property was purchased by Jews prior to 1920, as two 1917 letters from the Lummus Investment Co. to Isidor Cohen clearly show that Mr. Cohen was buying property north of Fifth Street in March and April of that year.

The Lummus brothers, J.N. and J.E., like Isidor Cohen, arrived in the Miami area in 1896 and became prominent on both sides of the bay. It appears, from what Marcia Zerivitz writes, that the Lummus brothers "had dealt with Jewish people before and were comfortable doing business with them."

Fisher, however, along with people such as Pancoast; Harvey Firestone; John H. Levi, his general manager and later mayor of Miami Beach; Pete Chase, his sales manager who had taken Doc Dammers's place; John Oliver LaGorce; and no few others, believed that the "loud and poorly dressed New York Jews" should not be permitted to purchase certain parcels of land, stay in many of the hotels that were operating on the beach side or belong to the private clubs that were being opened by Fisher and others in order to provide a haven from the type of people who Fisher and his associates deemed undesirable. Historically, it was the black eye of Greater Miami's religious history.

Although New York had passed the first state civil rights act forbidding racial or religious discrimination in 1899, Greater Miami had no such considerations of conscience. As the area grew, so did the restrictions on Jewish home ownership, rights to register as hotel guests or membership in certain private clubs. Jewish doctors and teachers were denied positions in hospitals and schools due to their religion, and it would not be until the mid- to late 1930s that concerted efforts were made to protest and overturn such blatant and vile discriminatory practices.

Among the anti-Semitic clubs were the Surf, Bath and LaGorce on Miami Beach, as well as Riviera Country Club in Coral Gables and a number of yacht clubs. Although Miami Shores Country Club, owned by the municipality, was not officially anti-Semitic, its reputation was that Jews were not welcome. Many years later, in the mid-1980s, the late and unlamented village manager Elly Johnson, who was imported from Alabama, regularly made anti-Semitic remarks in my presence, the dates, times and names of other individuals present being documented, bringing that vile specter back to life. Johnson was aided and abetted at the time by several village residents and three of five members of the village council, who, instead of voting to fire him for his unethical actions, blatant anti-Semitism and boorish behavior, voted to keep him in office, proving to the community that it would take more than legislation to eliminate bigotry.

Restricted hotels and apartment houses included, among many others, the Hampton Court, Hiawatha, Brisa del Mar, Linden, Indian Creek (which advertised "Gentiles Exclusively Solicited") and Helene Apartments, as well as the Mayflower (with one of it's selling points being "A Clientele that's 'Your Sort!'") and the Braznell Hotels, all on Miami Beach. In Sunny Isles the Green Heron Hotel and Pan American Motel excluded Jewish people, while in Bal Harbour the Kenilworth and Sea View Hotels did the same. Several properties, including the Clay Hotel at Espanola Way and Washington Avenue on Miami Beach, had signs on or in front of them that clearly stated "No Jews."

Equally as distasteful were the deed restrictions and covenants forbidding home or property owners to sell their premises to "persons of Semitic origin." These restrictive clauses existed in large areas of Miami Beach, including two of the Sunset Islands and all of LaGorce Island, all of Bal Harbour, parts of Miami Shores and Surfside, Indian Creek Island, Griffing's Biscayne Park Estates, Bay Point and likely other areas of Dade County.

In 1934, with the encouragement of the *Jewish Floridian* newspaper, Baron deHirsch Meyer became the first person of Jewish origin to be elected to the Miami Beach City Council. Within several years, Miami Beach became the home of a majority of Greater Miami's Jewish residents and the "balance of power" in the Jewish community began to shift to the beach side of Biscayne Bay.

In 1939, the storied Mitchell Wolfson, one of the founders of Wometco Enterprises, was elected to the beach council and in 1943 was elevated to the position of mayor, the first of his religion to serve in that capacity. Slowly but surely, "the times, they were inexorably a-changin'."

Although the influx of Jewish former servicemen following World War II would increase Greater Miami's population enormously, anti-Semitism continued to exist and would make its last public stand in the mid-1960s. At that time, several hotels on Miami Beach, in Bal Harbour and in Sunny Isles maintained their invalid right to discriminate until the Civil Rights Act of 1964 was upheld by the U.S. Supreme Court in 1965. The concept of restricted deed covenants survived, however, until the 1976 federal court ruling dealing with the sale of a home in Bal Harbour.

The court, in its landmark ruling, stated that while the concept of restrictive covenants was *not* illegal, the court would refuse to uphold them because such deed clauses prohibiting persons of certain religions or races from purchasing property were in direct violation of the public policy of the United States. It was with that ruling that the restricted covenant clause died an unlamented death.

Regretfully and unhappily, the practice of anti-Semitism did not die at the same time and a good amount of it remains intact in today's Miami-Dade County. Several institutions, including at least two private colleges in the county, actively engage in that foul and vile practice. In Miami Shores, the taint of a good few individuals who are no better than the old-time "redneck" and "cracker" bigots is a stain on the community, and until the poison of that anti-Semitism is destroyed once and for all—if it even or ever can be—the foul stench of discrimination, though not as open or blatant or even accepted as it once was, will continue to blight Greater Miami.

This page: As the reader will note in this chapter, there was almost no end to the couched terminology by which the various hospitality venues made it clear that those of the Hebrew faith were not welcome. The Abbott Court Apartments at 6838 Abbott Avenue simply placed the word "Restricted" on the back side of its postcard, while the letter sent to prospective guests by the Abbott Towers clearly states, in the paragraph above the rates, that they cater to a Christian clientele.

ABBOTT TOWERS

8035-8045 ABBOTT AVENUE • TEL. 86-2478
MIAMI BEACH, FLORIDA

MR. AND MRS. JAMES V. WARNOCK

Dear Vacationist,

Are you aware of the fact that you may have a new spacious apartment with hotel service, just 500 feet from the ocean, for the same price as a confining hotel room?

We offer both a studio apartment, which may accommodate two or three people; or a larger, livingroom-bedroom apartment that is ample for 2, 4 or even 5 guests. Hotel rooms are also available.

All sleeping accommodations are regular size twin beds. Dressing rooms, tiled baths, dinettes and complete kitchens, where meals or snacks may be prepared at will, or just the fact of having a refrigerator available for cool drinks, make our apartments desirable. Maid service, all linens and utilities are included in all apartments and hotel rooms as part of our service.

Free surf bathing directly from your rooms, and a patio where one may relax and sun bathe all go toward making Abbott Towers a delightful place to spend a holiday. (All apartments open on to the patio).

We cater to a Christian Clientele and are located in the exclusive North Beach section, a short walk from churches, restaurants, theatres, shops and bus lines.

DAILY TOURIST RATES - APRIL 1st on

Studio Apts. - $2.50 per day, per person (double occupancy)
Bedroom " - $3.00 " " " " " "
Hotel Room - $2.00 " " " " " "

WEEKLY RATES

Studio Apts. & Hotel Rooms - Accommodate 1, 2 or 3 guests.

April Rates	$ 30.00 up weekly for	2 persons
May to December Rates	25.00 " " "	2 "
January Rates	50.00 " " "	2 "
February "	85.00 " " "	2 "
March "	75.00 " " "	2 "

Small charge for third person

Bedroom & Living Room Apts. - Accommodate 2, 3 or 4 people.

April Rates	$ 40.00 up weekly for	2 persons
May to December Rates	35.00 " " "	2 "
January Rates	60.00 " " "	2 "
February "	125.00 to $150.00 "	2 "
March "	125.00 to $150.00 "	2 "

Special monthly rates on request.

This page The Archambo Hotel, at Forty-second Street and Indian Creek Drive, made certain, using the exact words, that those wishing to stay there knew the hotel was "Gentile owned and operated." The Arnold, at Eighty-eighth Street and Collins Avenue in Surfside, included the words "Gentile Clientele" on the cover of its promotional brochure.

This page: The Churchill on Collins Avenue and Thirty-sixth Street, the Duke at Harding Avenue and Eighty-third Street and the Coronado at Eighty-eighth Street and Collins Avenue had no qualms about placing "Gentile Clientele" on the covers of their brochures, while the Good Hotel at Forty-third Street and Collins Avenue introduced itself as "A Distinctive Hotel for Discriminating Guests."

This page: From the day it opened on Collins Avenue in Bal Harbour almost until the day it was torn down to be replaced by condos, the Kenilworth was restricted. Its owner in the mid-1950s, when he started doing his nationally televised variety show from the hotel, was Arthur Godfrey. Accusations of anti-Semitism shadowed Godfrey during the height of his career and persist today. Arthur J. Singer, in his 2000 biography of Godfrey, *The Adventures of an American Broadcaster*, rejects that accusation, citing Godfrey's good personal relations with a number of Jews in the entertainment industry, including his longtime announcer Tony Marvin. While that may have been true, the fact was that the Kenilworth remained restricted through all of the years of Godfrey's ownership, contrary to what Singer wrote in his book.

The brochure for the Carl Fisher–owned Lincoln Hotel (the hotel was on the southwest corner of Lincoln Road and Washington Avenue) states, "The Lincoln affords a quiet homelike place of residence catering only to a select and exclusive clientele and through its policies of operation has created an environment that has won the favor of discriminating guests." A following line in the brochure confirms the above, for the guest is asked to "please present recommendations."

Beautiful MAYFLOWER Restaurant
and Cocktail Room
OPEN ALL YEAR
Full Course Dinner from 75c
Lunch from 40c

FEATURES

Solarium Free to Our Guests
Large Airy Outside Rooms — Perfectly Appointed Rooms
Deep Feather-Soft Beds — 100 Rooms—90 Tubs and Showers
Full Length Mirrors in Every Room — Venetian Blinds
Telephones — Convenient to Everything
Elevators to All Floors — Outlet for Electric Razor
Open Air Patio for Dining and Dancing
Dress in Your Room for Surf Bathing

FREE AUTO PARKING
WRITE, WIRE OR PHONE 5-3323
FOR RESERVATIONS

The Beautiful Mayflower Hotel
offers you many things beside lodging.

A Location that suits you.

"Atmosphere" Congenial to you.

A type of service that you will like.

A clientele that's "your sort."

A friendly management.

A dignified address.

At the Desk to Greet You
HERBERT POTTS — WILLIAM CROCKETT
SPEARS FUTCH

One of my favorite terminologies was used by the Mayflower Hotel (later the Variety, now a condo) on the northwest corner of Seventeenth Street and Alton Road. As one of its selling points, the hotel advertised "Atmosphere Congenial to you," but that was overshadowed by the even more direct "A clientele that's 'your sort'!"

This page: While the Normandy Plaza stated its guest preference in relatively small letters, the Pierre, at Forty-third Street and Collins Avenue, made no bones about ensuring that potential guests knew who was and who was not welcome.

This page: Two more examples of brochure cover blatancy include the Ocean Grande and the Patrician, both using the "Gentile Clientele" terminology up front.

The Tackler

VOL. 6 JANUARY 1, 1936 NO. 1

8:30 P.M.

INSTALLATION NIGHT

RALPH I. VERVOORT DOING THE HONORS

CHAIRMAN J. HOLDEN BECKWITH

SPECIALTY ACTS

FREE BEER

The Rod and Reel Club
Hibiscus Island
Miami Beach, Florida

Among the restricted clubs was the Rod and Reel Club on the County (now MacArthur) Causeway. Jewish requests for membership were, as they were at the clubs named in the introduction to this chapter as well as at many other yacht and boating clubs, ignored or denied. It would not be until 1984 that the barriers against Rod and Reel Club membership for those of Jewish heritage were broken down. Early in the twenty-first century, Dan "Cap'n Dan" Kipnis, the club's first Jewish member, became its second Jewish president.

Bal Harbour's Sea View Hotel used the term "Selected Clientele" quite discreetly on its brochure.

J. N. LUMMUS, PRESIDENT | MITCHELL D. PRICE, VICE-PRESIDENT | JAMES COPE, SEC'Y-TREAS.

THE LUMMUS INVESTMENT COMPANY
CAPITAL $25,000.00

MIAMI BEACH, FLORIDA

April 4th,1917

RECEIVED of Isidor Cohen the sum of $100.00 part payment on lots in tract of land known as the Edmund Wilson Tract now being platted and subdivided. The purchase price to be $4600.00. Terms - $2200.00 on delivery of deed, balance on mortgage one, two and three years. Lots Nos. 7 to 12 inclusive in Block 3. The property has been purchased by John Friedman and James Cope from Edmund Wilson The deed has been prepared and forwarded to Edmund Wilson for signatures and a deed to Mr. Cohen will be executed by the Southern Bank & Trust Company, acting under power of attorney for John Friedman and James Cope as soon as the plat has been filed together with the deeds.

THE LUMMUS INVESTMENT COMPANY AG TS
By James Cope

This April 4, 1917 letter from Lummus Investment Company to Isidor Cohen provides proof that Jewish businessmen were able to purchase land north of Fifth Street on Miami Beach prior to 1920. (A previous letter dated March 30, 1917, from Mr. Cope to Mr. Cohen also confirms Mr. Cohen's purchase of other Miami Beach property north of Fifth Street.)

MARY H. GLEASON, PRESIDENT — EORGE W. GLEASON, VICE PRESIDENT — W. H. H. GLEASON, SECY. AND TREAS.

GLEASON BROTHERS & COMPANY

INCORPORATED 1899

REAL ESTATE AND LOANS

~~EAU GALLIE, FLORIDA~~ Miami Fla March 7 1924

Dear George.

I have your letter of the 5th in regard to selling the Miami Beach land, In regard to the $300.000.00 offer for it in bulk I looked into it and found that the offer was $250000.00 when I got them to put it in writing with $50.000.00 pay down and $50.000.00 a year until paid without interest. ,this I turned down,i wrote Lansing fully yesterday about all of the offers &c which I presume he has told you.

I do not think we should sell to Jews under any consideration.

I am enclosing Banlks for you to make your Mothers Income tax report also statememt of receipts and payments made during the year Classified so you can make the report,I have not put anything in this expedditures in the way of taxes or Insurance about the St Augustine place that you have.

I have not been feeling very well for the past few days so will not do much for the next two days and try and take in the races. Love to all

Afft Yours
Unk Will

At some point early in the twentieth century, William Gleason, after pioneering on the Miami River, moved to Eau Gallie, Florida, in Brevard County, while retaining a good bit of Miami-area land. In this March 7, 1924 letter, William's virulent anti-Semitism pours out as he writes, in the second paragraph of a letter to his nephew dealing with an offer to purchase land from the Gleasons by an unnamed party, "I do not think we should sell to Jews under any consideration."

Chapter Four

Buildings, Businesses and Stores

Isidor Cohen's book *Historical Sketches and Sidelights of Miami, Florida*, published in 1925, relates that he made his first Miami sale on February 11, 1896, just five days after his arrival. He implies that the Jacob Schneidman store or business was the next Jewish-owned sales outlet to open, but regretfully, there is no way to exactly date the openings of each Jewish merchant's business.

There were myriad retail stores, beginning, of course, with Cohen's and Schneidman's. By 1909, David Afremow opened the New York Bargain Store, later changing the word "Bargain" to "Department." Afremow eventually sold the building and business to brothers-in-law Daniel Cromer and Irwin Cassel, partners in the New York Department Store, which became Cromer Cassell in May 1926. After the store was sold, Daniel Cromer started a wholesale dry goods business that was eventually operated by his son Maurice and remains very much in business under the management of his grandson Daniel, with the current name of the Cromer Company.

In the automobile business, the Ungar (Buick), Spitzer (Dodge and Chrysler), Luby (Chevrolet) and Lehman (Buick) families would lead the way. Auto parts and repair would follow and among the Jewish-owned auto repair shops and tire stores were "Johnny and Mack by the railroad track—the world's largest and that's a fact!," Shorty and Fred's and Giant Motors, the latter two on Miami Beach. Norton Pallot Tire Company had stores throughout Greater Miami.

Jewish people were strong in the jewelry business, including Traveler's Luggage and Jewelry on Miami Avenue (William Rubin and son), Richter's, Mayors (the Getz family), Balough's, Freddy's (Shelley and Freddy Strauss), Kirk's (the Newbauer family) and many others.

The funeral and mortuary business has had its share of famous Jewish names, including Emanuel Gordon (who opened Miami's first Jewish funeral home on Southwest Twelfth Avenue in 1938), son Harry Gordon, grandson Jimmy Gordon and great-grandson, the late Craig Gordon; Eddie Newman (the first licensed Jewish funeral director in Florida); Irvin, Larry, Michael and Ira Blasberg; Sonny Levitt; Murray Rubin; and Leonard Zilbert.

The wholesale food purveyors included (again, among many others) Harry Diamond Wholesale Produce, Ruth and Albert Rosenberg of Miami Purveyors, Seymour Friend of Sanitary Fish, Pat Deare and Herman Pearl of Kosher Zion, Barney Rosenberg and Benard Rosenblatt of Collins Fish & Seafood, Harry Sturm of American Produce and Irving Karp of Carnival Fruit. Jewish-owned markets included Lobel's on Fifteenth Street and Washington Avenue, the Friedland family's Food Fair, the Thal Brothers (now the Starkman family's) Epicure Market, Bob's Fruit Market on Sixth Street and Thrifty Supermarket on South Beach.

Jewish people were strong in the baking business, and among the numerous shops and wholesale operations was the Goren family's bakery of that name on Southwest Eighth Street. Others included the Linksman family's Pumpernik's Bakery on Sixty-seventh Street on Miami Beach, Butterflake Bakery (retail), Hirsch and Chotiner's New York Bakery, Gelber's Bakery on Sixth Street between Meridian and Jefferson and Paramount Bakery. Bagels were supplied to most bakeries and restaurants by Beach Bagel, located for many years on Miami Beach, although later moved to Miami.

The Jewish interest in banks and banking included the legendary Broad family (American Savings); the Gaynor, Courshon and Giller families (Jefferson National Bank and Washington Federal); the Abess family (North Shore Bank and its successors); the Lipton family (Dade Federal); and the Carner family, as well as Albert Pallot and his nephew, Richard C. Schulman, and their Biscayne Federal. As with other businesses, a listing would take pages.

Construction was the province of the Justins, the Goldmans, the Turchins, the Arkins, Jerry Cohen, Leonard Miller of Lennar, Robert Merritt and a good few more. Simply put, a listing of Jewish-owned stores, buildings and businesses would require a sizable volume, as it would have to include sign shops (Jess Bramson's York Sign Co., Max Landesman of the sign company bearing his name, Mickey Krause of Claude Neon and Moe Bengis and Sam Dunst of Tropicalites), clothing stores, fur salons, shoe stores, travel agencies and every other kind and type of business known, including cable and connector manufacturing (Katherine and Ben Nemser's Nemal Electronics), trucking companies such as Alterman Trucking and Gold Coast and International Carriers (owned by Edwin and Danny Weintraub), aviation operations (Mickey and Sherman Tobin of Bonanza Aviation and Josh Nemser and his aunt, Saralyn Nemser, of Catalina Aerospace) and a large number of drugstores. Arthur and Larry Apple own Associated Photographers, one of the largest commercial photography businesses in America, and Jewish people did and do own strip shopping centers and entire shopping malls (the Sofer family, Aventura Mall). Obviously, these are just a miniscule few of the businesses and occupations in which the Jewish people of Greater Miami have been and are engaged.

Hyman (Hy, sometimes Harry) Diamond moved to Miami in 1930 and by 1933 was operating H. Diamond Wholesale Produce. Operating out of Knight's Market, Harry is shown here in his first truck, circa 1934. *Courtesy Hanna Diamond Lipton.*

Louis Pallot moved to Miami in 1924 and in 1926 opened his first tire store, acting as both salesman and tire changer. An incredibly rare view shows Louis standing inside the store with his stock, prior to his founding of Norton Pallot Tire Co. *Courtesy Barbara Pallot Katzen.*

A very rare late 1930s view of Flagler Street looking west from just east of Northeast Second Avenue shows, at right, Cowen's store with Harry the Hatter just on the other side of it. Harry and the Rippa family were chapeau suppliers to individuals and businesses in Miami and the rest of Florida for years. Farther west on Flagler, the sign on top of the Shepard Broad–owned Biscayne Building, far right, is quite visible.

Above: Avenue D and Eleventh Street was the corner of Miami Avenue and Northeast First Street by the time this G.W. Romer photo was made in 1925. Prominent at left is the New York Department Store sign, the names Cromer & Cassel appearing immediately below the word "Store."

Right: By the early 1930s, the appearance of the street had changed dramatically. Looking north on Miami Avenue from Flagler Street, the first prominent sign on the right is that of William Rubin & Son Luggage and Jewelry, while immediately north, across Northeast First Street, is Cromer Cassel's.

Always a great favorite with carbonated beverage drinkers, 7-Up has long been popular in Miami. Owned by the Tobin family, the plant at 3730 North Miami Avenue is shown here *Courtesy Sherman Tobin.*

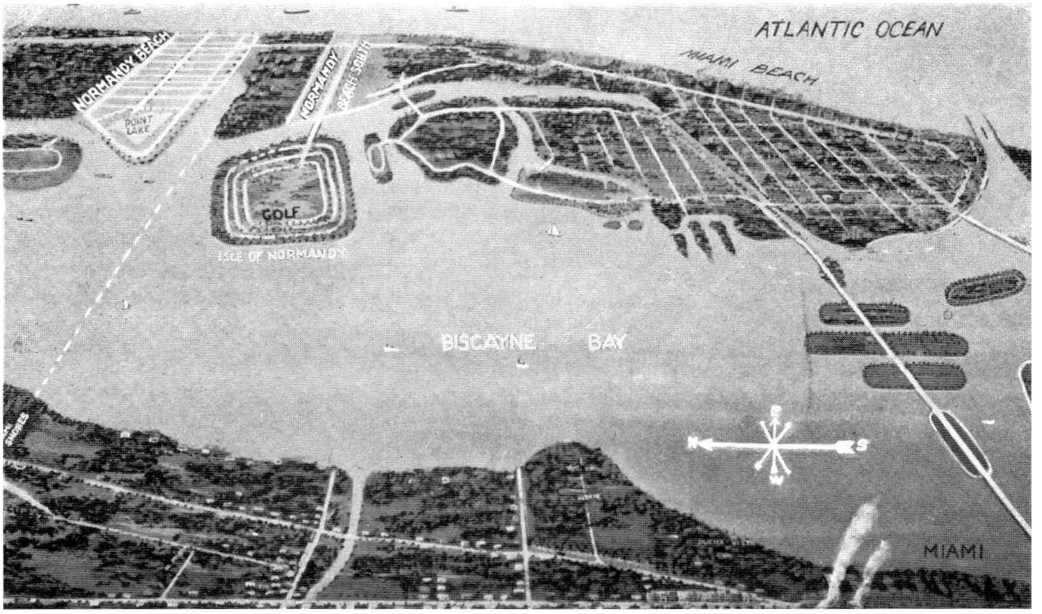

One of Miami's greatest and yet one of the most under-remarked developers was Henri (Henry) Levy, who built Normandy Isle and the lower third of Surfside. Shown here is the Normandy Beach Properties promotional card, which indicated the site of the not-yet-completed Normandy Isle as well as Normandy Beach, which was the first part of what would become Surfside.

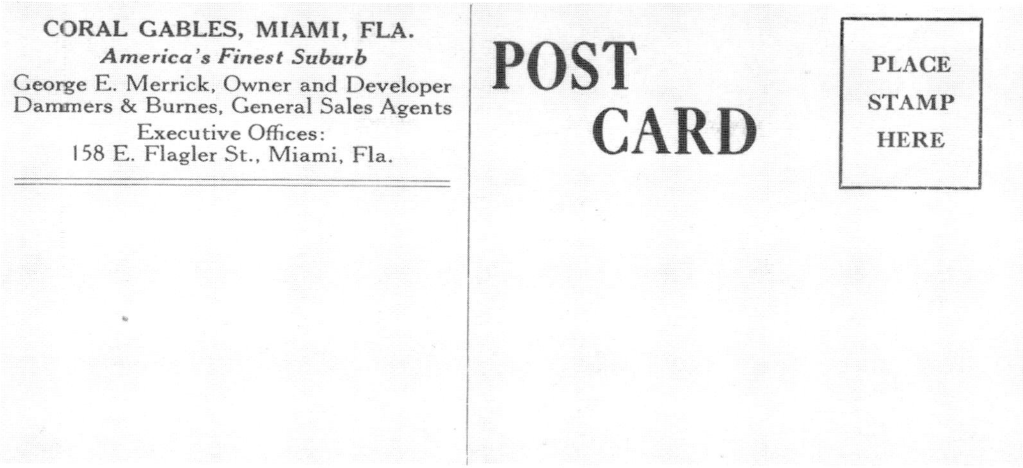
CORAL GABLES, MIAMI, FLA.
America's Finest Suburb
George E. Merrick, Owner and Developer
Dammers & Burnes, General Sales Agents
Executive Offices:
158 E. Flagler St., Miami, Fla.

POST CARD

PLACE STAMP HERE

Jewish property developers and entrepreneurs have been associated with Miami since its earliest years. One of the most historically renowned is Dr. Edward E. "Doc" Dammers, who, as previously noted, was George Merrick's right-hand man, sales director and first mayor of Coral Gables. This, the back of a Merrick Coral Gables "gold" postcard, notes that Dammers and Burnes (his partner) were general sales agents for Merrick.

H.H. "Dad" Farr was the first Jewish travel agent in Miami. With his two sons, Aaron and Bill, H.H. pioneered innumerable travel agency innovations, including tours over Miami and Miami Beach by air, as shown by the poster attached to the desk that is facing the camera. In this 1930 photograph in the first Farr Tours office, H.H., behind the desk on the left, is concluding a transaction. The framed steamship photos on the walls would be, if still extant, worth several thousand dollars each! *Courtesy Myra Farr.*

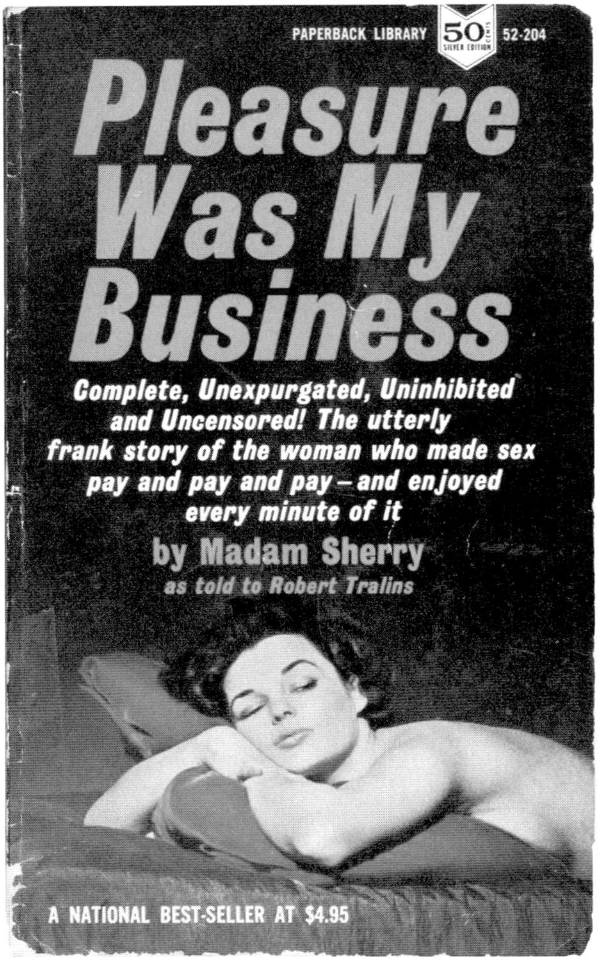

She unquestionably ran one of the best—if not *the* best—big whorehouses in Miami and the South. Her business name was Madam Sherry, and she operated in Miami from 1929 until the mid-1950s. Her largest and most lavish establishment was the Moorish Palace at 5400 Northeast Fourth Avenue, which was closed by the army in 1943, although she continued in business in other locations. Madam Sherry, according to the arduous research done by architect Antolin Carbonell, RA, was born Rebecca Levitch in 1893 and was the daughter of Leah and Robert Levitch, who operated a secondhand store in St. Louis. Although she went through a supposed conversion to Christianity early in World War II, the fact is that she was born Jewish and used her sisters' names—Anne, Rose and Ruth—as her aliases. State attorney Richard Gerstein, grandstanding as he was infamous for doing, pretended he was in Boston and attempted to ban her book, *Pleasure Was My Business*, from being sold in Miami and in Florida when it was first published in 1961. He proclaimed that it violated community morals, which was so ludicrous, nonsensical and totally false that in 1964 the U.S. Supreme Court, in *Tralins v. Gerstein*, threw out the ban and admonished Gerstein severely. Shown here, *Pleasure Was My Business* is a fascinating look at Miami's—and Madam Sherry's—history.

An aerial view, looking south on November 28, 1953, shows the Moorish Palace at the corner of Northeast Fifty-fourth Street and Fourth Avenue. Biscayne Boulevard is the wide street at far left. The street paralleling the FEC Railway tracks is Federal Highway. The street crossing the tracks is Northeast Fifty-fourth Street and the first street on the right side of the tracks is Northeast Fourth Avenue, Madam Sherry's clearly visible at that intersection. Madam Sherry had been out of that location for ten years when this photo was taken, but she continued in business in Miami until the mid-1950s.

Above: Epicure is one of Greater Miami's foremost gourmet markets. Originally located on Washington Avenue on Miami Beach, the store was purchased in 1945 by the Thal Brothers and moved to Alton Road, where it thrives today under the direction of Ike and Jason Starkman. *Courtesy Historical Association of Southern Florida.*

Left: Tripure Water, one of the earliest of the healthy and pure bottled waters, was owned by Isaac and Robert A. Levin, who first arrived in Miami in the late 1920s. The phone number on the label—"2-4128"—indicates that the bottling plant was in Hialeah. *Courtesy Dorothy and Dr. Maurice Serotta.*

A number of Jewish families, including the Siegels, Leblangs and Zilbers, have been involved in the local passenger transportation business for many years. Among their properties have been American Sightseeing and Yellow Cab, a modern taxi of the latter company shown here.

In the early 1950s, Edward Weintraub built this gas station and truck service center at Northwest 103rd Street and 7th Avenue. Known at the time as the Seventh Avenue Truck Terminal, it was for many years one of Miami's largest truck servicing facilities. *Courtesy Danny Weintraub.*

In late 1957, Weintraub took over a struggling operation known as Gold Coast Truck Rental and within a short time had combined it with two other companies and built it into the giant International Carriers. The two men at left are unknown. The man in the center is Jim Riley, while the man fourth from left is unknown. The young man at far right is Edward's son, Danny. *Courtesy Danny Weintraub.*

Irving Jacobs may have had the first Jewish-owned service station in Dade County, at Sixth Street and Euclid Avenue on Miami Beach. This photograph appears to have been taken circa 1929 or '30. *Courtesy the Hauser family.*

Ungar Buick, which was Greater Miami's first Jewish-owned automobile dealership, issued this twofold, three-panel brochure for the introduction of the 1950 Buicks at their showroom, then located at 1201 Northeast Second Avenue. *Courtesy Marcella Werblow.*

In 1948, Ralph Renick, a young University of Miami broadcast journalism student, convinced Colonel Wolfson to allow him to begin television broadcasting from the former Capitol Theater at 306 North Miami Avenue. WTVJ became Florida's first television station and Renick, shown here, was the station's news anchor and a fixture in Greater Miami's homes for close to thirty years. His marvelous, deep voice and his trademark, "Good night and may the good news be yours," remain the hallmark of local broadcasting, which, to this day, no local broadcaster has attained or achieved. *Courtesy Historical Association of Southern Florida.*

This page: 710 Southwest Twelfth Avenue was originally the home of Freddie Diamond. By 1946, however, the Gordon family had purchased the property and opened the first Jewish funeral home in Greater Miami. The home, before and after conversion, is shown here. *Both images courtesy Jim Gordon.*

This page: Two of Miami Beach's favorite drugstores and pharmacies, along with Schrager's, were the Newman family's Penway at the corner of Espanola Way and Pennsylvania Avenue near Miami Beach High and Ben Grenalds' Moderne Drugs on Forty-first Street, a favorite spot for the kids from North Beach Elementary School and Nautilus Junior High, as they would gather there for their French fries, hamburgers and cherry, lemon and chocolate Cokes in the days of drugstore lunch counters. *Penway photo courtesy Sheldon Miller; Moderne Drugs photo courtesy Ben Grenald.*

Stone's Drugs was another of Ben Grenald's approximately fourteen drugstores and served the overtown area of black Miami, located on Northwest Second Avenue between Ninth and Tenth Streets. *Courtesy Ben Grenald.*

In September 1963, Governor George Wallace of Alabama visited the Kasdin Drug Store at 6625 Collins Avenue in the Deauville Hotel. While the names of the two women on either end are unknown, the pharmacist is Max Lerner and the lady between Messrs. Lerner and Wallace is Mrs. Ann Martin, mother of Miami Beach High graduate Ann Martin Schneider, now of Atlanta. *Courtesy Ann Martin Schneider.*

Leo Galvan was a contractor in Greater Miami for many years. Most of his work was done in Hialeah, where he lived and founded Temple Tifereth Jacob. Shown here, circa 1954, is his office at 7033 Northwest Thirty-sixth Avenue. *Courtesy Ella Galvan.*

This pcge: One of America's most celebrated architects, and like Norman Giller an accomplished author is Barry Sugerman. Among Sugerman's stunning home designs and architectural triumphs are the Weiss home and the Palenzuela residence, shown on this page.

A beautiful movie house, Wometco's Carib Theater on Lincoln Road, with its goldfish pond and macaws in the lobby, is warmly remembered. *Courtesy Sheldon Miller.*

Chapter Five

The Schools and the Temples

In 1912, in addition to the purchase of cemetery space in the city cemetery, twelve Jewish residents met for the purpose of organizing Miami's first temple, which they named B'nai Zion, honoring founder Morris Zion. In 1913, a YMHA (Young Men's Hebrew Association) was opened and by 1915 the approximately fifty Jews (it is uncertain if this was the number of individuals or the number of Jewish families) in Miami had decided to construct a synagogue.

In 1917, Temple B'nai Zion was reorganized and received its charter as Temple Beth David. Among the founders were Philip Ullendorf as president and Dan Cromer of the aforementioned Cromer-Cassel store. The initial site for the new temple was to be the southeast corner of Avenue B and Fourth Street (today's Northeast Second Avenue and Eighth Street), but due to World War I construction halted and the congregation traded the lot for a building at Avenue H and Tenth Street (today's Northwest Fourth Avenue and Second Street), which they then remodeled to suit their needs.

There are, in Miami-Dade County today, at least fifty-nine temples, synagogues and houses of Jewish worship of numerous and various persuasions within the religion, from the very liberal to the ultra orthodox. At the close of this chapter, the listing of those institutions as of 2008 (5768–69 on the Hebrew calendar) is shown.

In addition to the various temples offering Hebrew school classes, it appears that the first formal institution of and for Jewish learning in South Florida was the Hebrew Academy, which initially opened its doors in February of 1947 at 1 Lincoln Road, which was then the YMHA building.

Six first-grade youngsters were enrolled and by early March a kindergarten and pre-kindergarten class of sixteen children was in full swing. Dr. Sandy Andron, son of the first president, Dr. David S. Andron, was one of six students in the highest grade, the fourth, and in fact had the first bar mitzvah at the Hebrew Academy. Other students were Mel Saks, Jerry Rabinowitz, Jerome Herman, Rose Berman and Moshe Shapiro. Five more first graders enrolled during the semester and at the end of the school term, nine children were ready to enter the second grade.

In May 1947, Aaron S. Lauer, Dr. David Andron and the late Harry Levitt, acting on behalf of the academy, purchased the building located at Sixth Street and Jefferson Avenue, which then housed a Methodist church, for $45,000. In December 1947, Rabbi Alexander S. Gross arrived in Miami, and in January of 1948 he dedicated the building. The school remained on Sixth Street until 1963 when, with a burgeoning enrollment, it was moved to the new campus at Dade Boulevard and Pine Tree Drive on Miami Beach.

Among the Jewish-owned private schools were Abbott Gardens, Lear, Normandy and Manheimer, and for many years the predominance of Jewish students at Miami Beach High made it seem as if that school was a prep school as well, its students routinely going to the Ivy Leagues as well as schools such as Georgia Tech, Vanderbilt, Tulane, Duke, Brandeis, Berkeley, Southern Cal, University of Chicago and many others. The list of the school's graduates reads like a who's who in American medicine, jurisprudence, business, government, education, science and the arts, and for many years Beach High was, with the singular exception of Bronx High School of Science, the number one rated academic public high school in America.

Shown here is a 1940 view of the original school, known from its opening in the late 1920s until 1935 as Ida M. Fisher High School, named in honor of the mother of the founder of Miami Beach. In 1936, the first class graduated from the newly renamed Miami Beach High School. *Courtesy Sherman Tobin.*

This page: A number of area private schools were operated by Jewish headmasters, including the Lear School at 1010 West Avenue, Miami Beach (later at 113th Street and Biscayne Boulevard on the Miami side), and Abbott Gardens Private School at 7705 Abbott Avenue, Miami Beach, owned by Yetta and Harold Malamud.

Robert E. Lee Jr. High School

Miami, Florida

Code of Honor Award

This Certifies That, *the Faculty and Students of the School, organized to advance the interest of the Students in school loyalty and pride, commend*

Dorothy Levin

for high qualities of scholarship, Civic Habits, Participation, and Character. The honor medal is awarded by the Student Council.

1ST YEAR HONOR MEDAL

2ND YEAR HONOR MEDAL

3RD YEAR HONOR MEDAL

Above: Dorothy Levin, while living in Miami, attended Robert E. Lee Junior High. In her ninth-grade year in the mid-1930s, Dorothy was presented with the Code of Honor award for the third time. *Courtesy Dorothy Serotta.*

Fourth Annual

Commencement

Ida M. Fisher High School

MIAMI BEACH
FLORIDA

F

HIGH SCHOOL AUDITORIUM
WEDNESDAY, JUNE 4, 1930
8:00 P. M.

Left: Ida M. Fisher High School retained that name until 1935. The following year, Fisher became a junior high school and Miami Beach High came into existence. In 1930 Milton Weiss, who would later marry CeeCee Alexander, graduated from "Ida M." *Courtesy Alexa Weiss Rossy.*

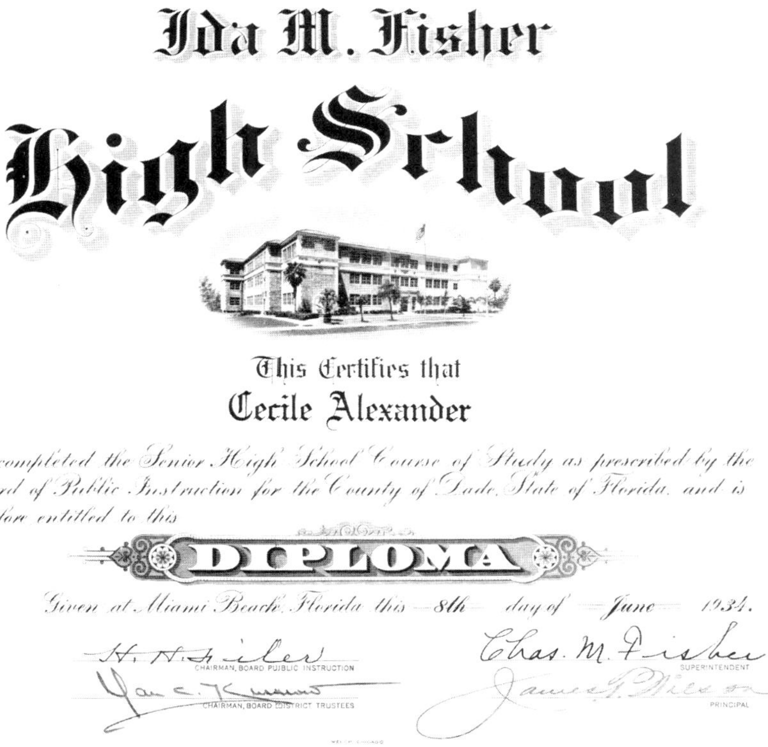
Ida M. Fisher
High School

This Certifies that
Cecile Alexander
has completed the Senior High School Course of Study as prescribed by the Board of Public Instruction for the County of Dade, State of Florida, and is therefore entitled to this
DIPLOMA
Given at Miami Beach, Florida this 8th day of June 1934.

CHAIRMAN, BOARD PUBLIC INSTRUCTION
SUPERINTENDENT
CHAIRMAN, BOARD DISTRICT TRUSTEES
PRINCIPAL

Above: Cecile (CeeCee) Alexander graduated from Fisher in 1934, in the next to last class to graduate prior to the school being renamed Miami Beach Senior High. *Courtesy Alexa Weiss Rossy.*

Right: A 1953 Miami Beach High football program for that year's game against Coral Gables. *Courtesy Barbara and Barry Sugerman.*

The

HEBREW ACADEMY

NEWS

SEPTEMBER, 1961 ELLUL 5721

At Long Last

After seven long years of battle with overwhelming forces which kept us confined to our old and inadequate quarters on Sixth Street, we have finally, with the aid of the Almighty, begun construction of our new buildings on Pine Tree Drive and 24th Street. As of this writing, the foundation is being laid, and soon enough we shall see the structure rise.

This did not come easy. Much pain, heartache and hard work were the ingredients that brought us to this level of success. The sacrificial devotion of a handful of men and women who never flinched or slackened their efforts served to inspire countless others who otherwise may have wavered. Never have so few done so much for the advancement of Torah education in our community.

Our heartfelt appreciation and genuine thanks are here extended to the contributors and workers in our Campaign. Extra special thanks, however, go to the members of hte Building Committee, whose ceaseless efforts have put us on the road to construction. These are the men, who behind the scenes, labored tirelessly:

Leonard Rosen, Chairman
Jerome Bienenfeld
Charles Charcowsky
Irving Firtel
Harry Genet
Maurice Goldring
Louis Merwitzer
Samuel Reinhard
Maurice Revitz

Let us keep pulling together until the job is completed. Ours will be the privilege and "Zechus" to raise the level of Torah and Jewish leadership in our community to the highest degree of accomplishment.

Welcome!

The need for a news media to keep abreast of the many and varied activities eminating from the school, the Hebrew Academy Women and the PTA, has long been felt.

The need becomes all the more urgent as the construction of our new buildings moves forward at a rapid pace. To be informed of the progress we are making is the first requirement for more active participation by all of us.

We welcome the Hebrew Academy News and hope that it will spur us all on to greater accomplishments.

As we approach the New Year, let us pray that it will be a happy and healthy year for all of us and that it will see the fulfillment of all our dreams.

B. I. BINDER, President.

Campaign Report

We are happy to report that we have close to $800,000 in pledges towards our Million Dollar Building Campaign goal. Chase Federal and Miami Beach Federal have jointly granted us a construction loan of $500,000, with the understanding that we are to raise an additional $300,000 in cash to make up the difference between the construction loan and the construction costs.

We now have cash in the bank, $125,000. We need an additional $175.000. This money is needed NOW to guarantee that there will be no interruption in the construcction.

This is the time when you can do us the most good. This is the time when all your love and devotion to the Hebrew Academy can be translated into concrete action. You can now, by turning your love into dollars, make the building go up.

Send us your check on the pledge you made, whether you made a previous payment on your pledge or not.

You help us now and the good Lord will help you on the New Year with health, happiness and prosperity.

LOUIS MERWITZER,
Campaign Chairman;

LEONARD ROSEN,
Building Committee Chairman.

The September 1961 edition of the *Hebrew Academy News* announced that construction had begun on the new facility and campus, which would open seventeen blocks north of the Sixth Street building in 1963.

This page: At the old school a group of happy children is smiling in the sunshine, but change was coming and the new, modern and beautiful Alexander S. Gross Hebrew Academy was a major event for Jewish education in all of south Florida.

"Holocaust Survivors"
Residing In Sunny Isles Beach
Temple B'nai Zion • Sunday, March 28, 2004

MICHAEL ACKER
ESSIA ACKER
AL ACKERSTEIN
JERRY ALEXANDER
LOUIS BENDER
BELLA BENDER
HELEN BERGER
JOSEPH BERGER
JOSEPH BIENENFELD
FREIDA BIENENFELD
BETTY BIRENBAUM
JOSEPH BIRNBAUM
REGINNA BLANK
MAX BLANK
ERNEST BOHN
HANNA BOHN
ESTERE BRAJZBLAT
FELICIA BRYN
RABBI NATHAN BRYN
ADELA BURSTYN
GEORGE BURSTYN
RUTH BURSTYN
MARTHA CHESTERSON
ROSE CHRUSTOWSKI
RACHEL CYPKIN
BARRY DAVIS
DORIS DIMITRIO
ISRAEL DIMITRIO
JOSEPH DOBRYMAN
NETTIE DOBRYMAN
RALPH DOLTON
EDWARD EDELSTEIN
MIRIAM EINSTEIN
JACK EISMAN
MARC EMMER
SAM FAIVISH
ANNA FAIWLOWICZ
NATHAN FEDER
LOUIS FEIG
LILLY FEIG
RAY FEIGENBLATT
CLARA FELDMAN
TIBOR FELDMAN
FRANCIS FINKELSTEIN
BERNARD FINN
BEN FREID
TAMARA FREID
LEON FULERO
FANI FULERO
ED FURMANSKI
ROSEW FURMANSKI
IVAN GABOR
SAM GASSON
SUSAN GASSON
SAMUEL GERSTENFELD
MEYER GINDIN
RAYA GINDIN
EMANUEL GINSBERG
RUBEN GLASS
FRANCES GOLD
JACOB GOLE
SARA GOLE
AARON GOPMAN
MIRIAM GOPMAN
IRENE GOTLIBOWICZ
PAULA GOTTLIEB
MORRIS GROSSMAN
RACHEL GWOZDINSKI
DANIEL HENDLER
MIRIAM HENDLER
BERTA HERMAN
SARA HERSKOVITZ
INGRID HESS
RITA HOFRICHTER
LOUIS HOFSTATTER
SALLY HORN
ANNA HOWSER
CY JOSEPH
MALA JOSEPH
FLORENCE KALINSKI
LOLA KAROL
HENRY KAY
SOL KAYE
JEAN KAYE
ABRAHAM KEIZMAN
FRIEDA KEIZMAN
REGINA KESTENBAUM
SALTSMAN
ABE KLAFTER
RACHEL KLAFTER
IDA KLINICKI
KATHE KOLIN
BARBARA KOPERWAS
ISRAEL KORN
PAULA KORN
EVA KOSTOW

Sunny Isles Beach has done much to honor survivors of the Holocaust. Under the direction of Mayor Norman Edelcup, the commission and event chairman Richard C. Schulman, the city honored all residents who were Holocaust survivors at a luncheon in that city on Sunday, March 28, 2004.

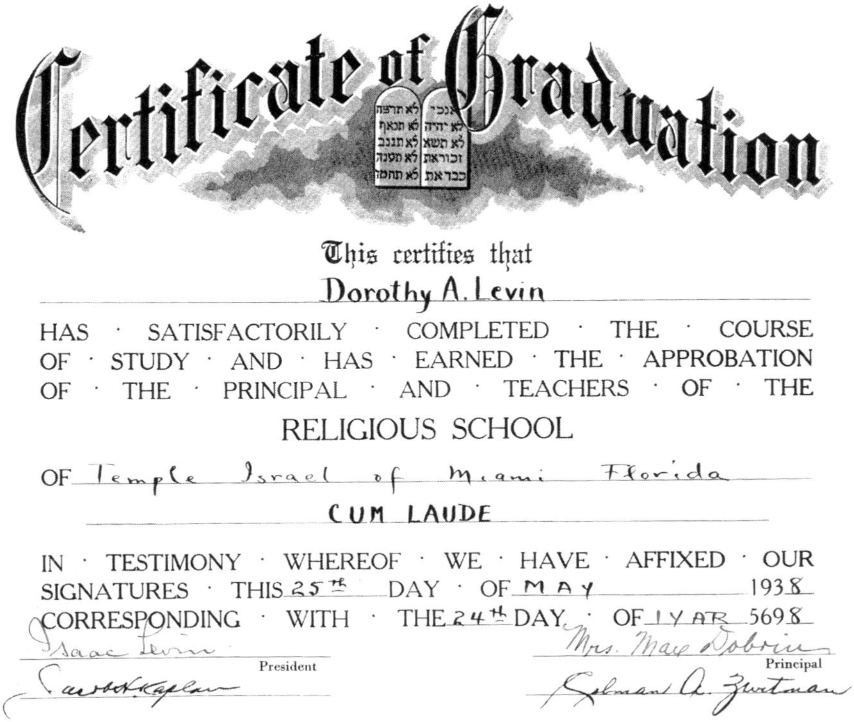

Certificate of Graduation

This certifies that

Dorothy A. Levin

HAS · SATISFACTORILY · COMPLETED · THE · COURSE OF · STUDY · AND · HAS · EARNED · THE · APPROBATION OF · THE · PRINCIPAL · AND · TEACHERS · OF · THE

RELIGIOUS SCHOOL

OF Temple Israel of Miami Florida

CUM LAUDE

IN · TESTIMONY · WHEREOF · WE · HAVE · AFFIXED · OUR SIGNATURES · THIS 25th DAY · OF MAY 1938 CORRESPONDING · WITH · THE 24th DAY · OF IYAR 5698

Isaac Levin — President

Mrs. Max Dobrin — Principal

Temple Israel, founded in 1922, celebrated its eighty-fifth anniversary in 2008, which was actually its eighty-sixth year, but at that age, who's counting?! The temple was originally just north of what is now the performing arts center opera house on Northeast Fourteenth Street and Biscayne Boulevard. When the boulevard was extended north the temple, which was on two lots beginning on the west side of the intersection of what is now Biscayne Boulevard and Fourteenth Street, was moved to its present location at 137 Northeast Nineteenth Street. In 1934, only twelve years after the temple's founding, Dorothy A. Levin graduated cum laude from the temple's religious school. Her certificate of completion is shown here. *Courtesy Dorothy Serotta.*

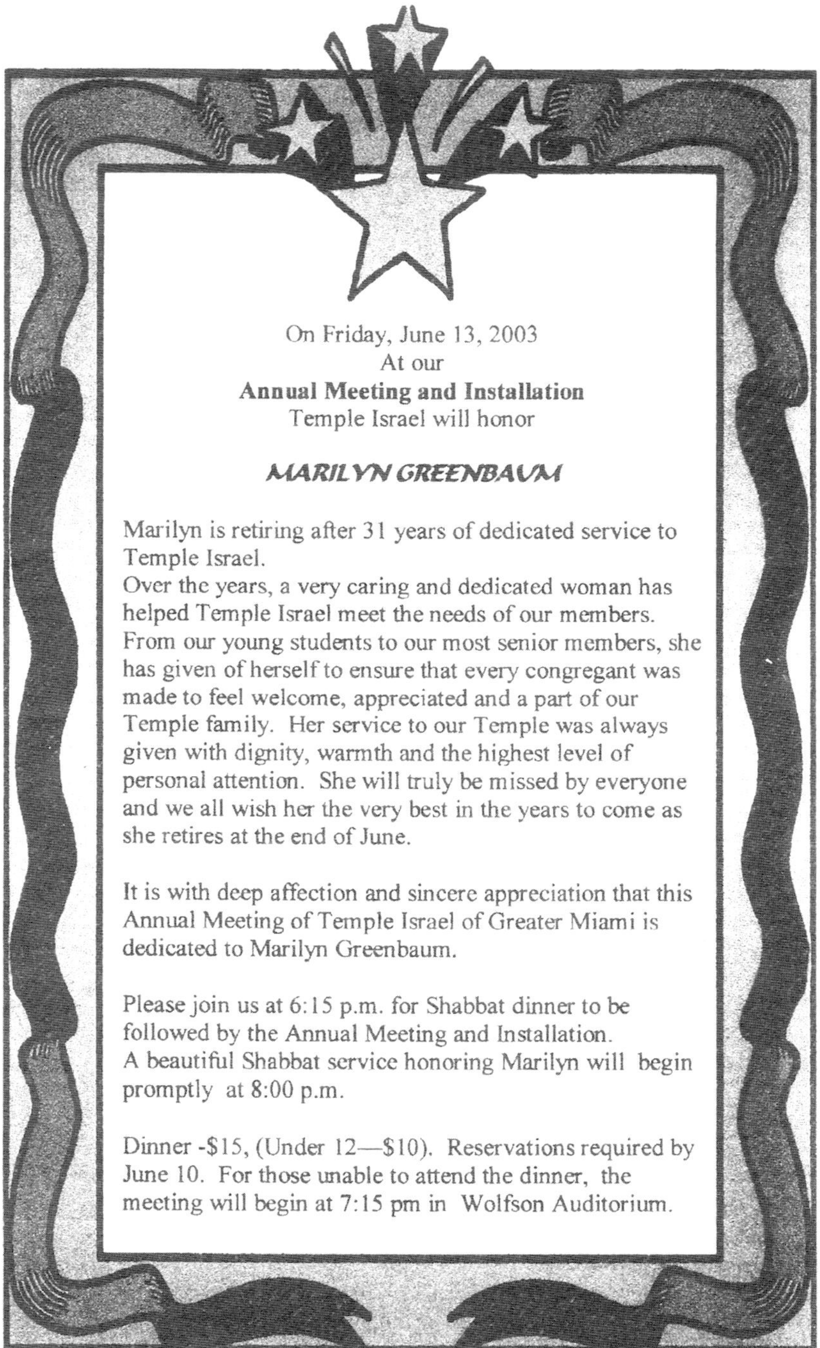

On Friday, June 13, 2003
At our
Annual Meeting and Installation
Temple Israel will honor

MARILYN GREENBAUM

Marilyn is retiring after 31 years of dedicated service to Temple Israel.
Over the years, a very caring and dedicated woman has helped Temple Israel meet the needs of our members. From our young students to our most senior members, she has given of herself to ensure that every congregant was made to feel welcome, appreciated and a part of our Temple family. Her service to our Temple was always given with dignity, warmth and the highest level of personal attention. She will truly be missed by everyone and we all wish her the very best in the years to come as she retires at the end of June.

It is with deep affection and sincere appreciation that this Annual Meeting of Temple Israel of Greater Miami is dedicated to Marilyn Greenbaum.

Please join us at 6:15 p.m. for Shabbat dinner to be followed by the Annual Meeting and Installation.
A beautiful Shabbat service honoring Marilyn will begin promptly at 8:00 p.m.

Dinner -$15, (Under 12—$10). Reservations required by June 10. For those unable to attend the dinner, the meeting will begin at 7:15 pm in Wolfson Auditorium.

This and opposite page: The June 13, 2003 issue of Temple Israel *Chai Lites* noted, on its cover, the retirement of Marilyn Greenbaum after thirty-one years of service. On the back cover, several people who have been instrumental in providing photographs and/or information for this book are named, including Dorothy and Maurice Serotta and Marcella Werblow. *Courtesy Dorothy and Dr. Maurice Serotta.*

Special Thanks to:

- **Michael Orovitz,** for participating in tonight's service.
- **Dorothy & Maurice Serotta,** for opening the Ark, in honor of their 60th Anniversary.
- **Marcella Werblow**, for sponsoring Bimah Flowers in memory of Leonard Abess and Marcella Unger.
- **The Neufeld Family**, for sponsoring Bimah Flowers in honor of the 60th Anniversary of Dr. Maurice and Dorothy Serotta and the 2003 Confirmation/Affirmation Class.

Announcements:

- This week's **Rabbi's Fund** donated to Godmothers/Godfathers Religious School Support.
- **Saturday, June 7, 9:30 a.m. Shabbat Study followed by Shabbat Service.** New format and new room: Kahn Room.
- **Sunday, June 8. No Religious School.**
- **Friday, June 13, 6:30 p.m.** Come to Friday Night Services either at 6 p.m. or 8:00 p.m. At 6:15 p.m. Shabbat Dinner by **RESERVATION ONLY**. Call Phyllis by **12 noon on Thursday, June 12.** **At 7:15 p.m. Annual Meeting and New Board of Trustees Installation.**

Upcoming Events and Programs:

- **Pride Seder**. Join Ru'ach for this special celebration on June 18, at 6:00 P.M. The guest speaker will be Rabbi Sue Levi Elwell. RSVP at (305) 573-5900.
- **International Shabbat Dinners, on Friday, June 20, will feature the Jews in India. Ruth Rosenwasser** will speak the same night at Oneg Shabbat, about her research of Indian Jewish communities. RSVP at (305) 573-5900.
- **Feed the Homeless** will meet on Monday, June 23, 2003, at 3:00 p.m. at the Homeless Assistance Center, 1550 N. Miami Avenue.

Above: With the takeover of Cuba by the Castro dictatorship, a large number of Jewish families immigrated to Miami and opened several temples in the area. Shown at a bar mitzvah at the Cuban-American Congregation on Miami Beach in 1999 are, from left, Dr. Melvyn Sherman, Adam Citrin, Spencer C. Moore and Phyllis Sherman. *Courtesy Jeri-Sue Moore.*

Opposite above: Any bar or bat mitzvah is a joyous event. Shown here at the bar mitzvah of Craig Alter at Temple Emanu-El are, from left, Rabbi Farber, Ronald Alter, Craig, Margie Alter (Margie's grandfather was one of the founders of Westview Country Club), Rabbi Irving Lehrman and Cantor Elliot Dicker. *Courtesy Margie and Ron Alter.*

Opposite below: New Beth Tov Ahavot Shalom Men's Club President Dr. Abe Lavender, founder of the Miami Beach Historical Association and professor of sociology and Sephardic studies at Florida International University, in front of the temple in May 2008. *Courtesy Dr. Abe Lavender.*

TEMPLE BETH TOV
AHAVAT SHALOM

At this December 2002 Men's Club function at the temple, Rabbi Manuel Armon is in the center of the photo with tie and jacket on while Lou Fine, with his hand raised, is immediately to the right of the rabbi. Lou's wife, Dorothy, is to Lou's left. *Courtesy Phil Spool.*

There is a great closeness among members in the smaller temples and, from left, Ann Wisotsky, Shirley Harris, Dorothy Kobritz, Shirley Goldenberg, Norman Zwidel and Zelma Zwidel act as the kitchen crew for a Beth Tov Ahavot Shalom function. *Courtesy Phil Spool.*

Above: The magnificent new sanctuary of Beth David Congregation on Coral Way in Miami is shown shortly before its formal opening, with the windows open and the air conditioning not yet installed. Beth David is the direct lineal descendant of Miami's first congregation, B'nai Zion.

Right: The stunning Torah ark and lectern at Beth David's chapel, designed by the talented and highly regarded interior designer Rosalind Merritt. The chapel's architect, Peter Blitstein, also designed the most recent addition to Joe's Stone Crabs Restaurant, while Merritt's father, Robert, was contractor for the 1962 addition to Joe's. *Courtesy Rosalind Merritt.*

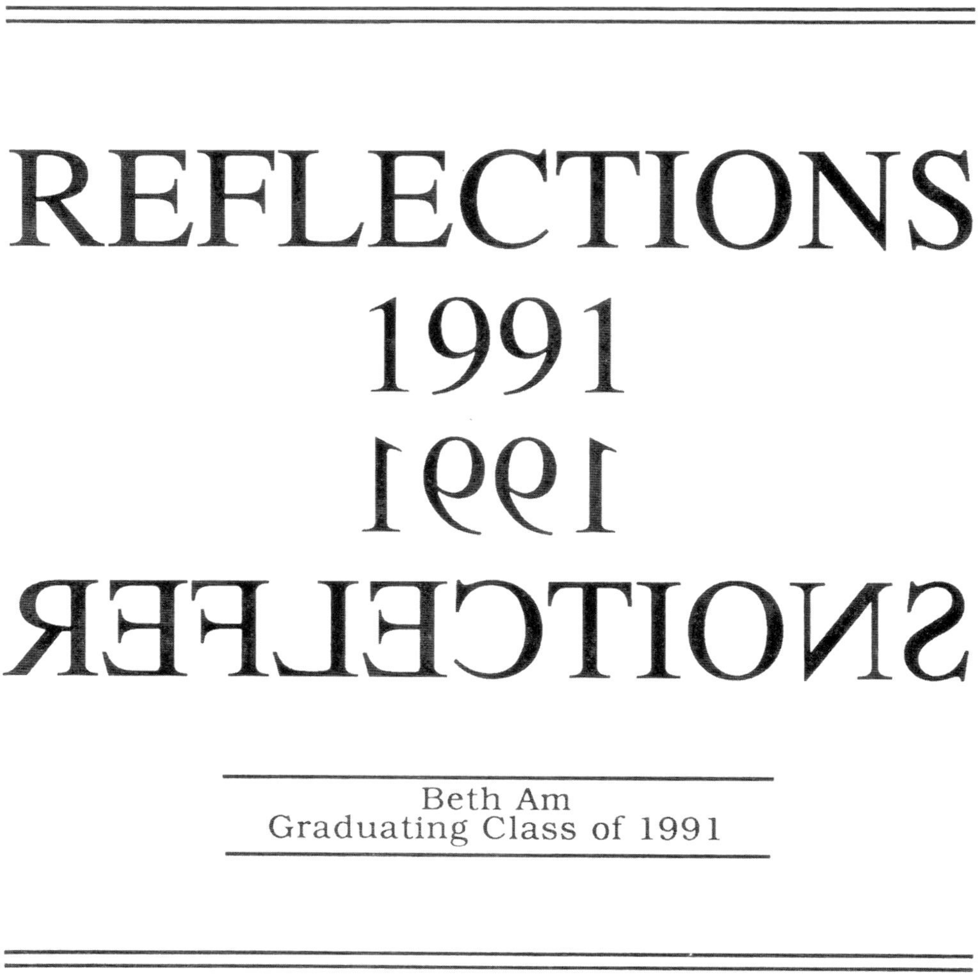

This and oppoite page: Temple Beth Am, at 5950 North Kendall Drive, serves southwest Miami-Dade. Shown here are two published pieces from the temple: the 1991 *Reflections* book, which listed all of that year's sixth-grade graduates, and the beautiful full-color booklet published by the temple to acquaint new members with its facilities and services. Reflections *booklet courtesy Mary Rose Kaplan; temple descriptive booklet courtesy Temple Beth Am.*

THE HOLY ARK

(Aron Hakodesh)

Temple Beth Am

5950 N. KENDALL DRIVE

(Southwest 88th St.)

MIAMI, FLORIDA 33156

PROGRAM OF ACTIVITIES

THE NEW

TEMPLE BETH MOSHE

DR. JOSEPH A. GORFINKEL
Rabbi

BETH MOSHE

13630 West Dixie Highway
North Miami, Florida 33161
Phone: 751-7578
891-5508

(temporary address)

This and opposite page: In 1949, North Dade Jewish Center was organized, followed by Temple Beth Emeth in 1955. In 1964, the temples merged to form Beth Moshe Congregation at 13630 West Dixie Highway. In 1972, the new school was built at 2225 Northeast 122nd Street, followed by the opening of the sanctuary in 1975, at which time the congregation moved to the new location. In 1998, Temple Ner Tamid, which had been located on Carlyle Avenue in Miami Beach, merged into Beth Moshe. In 1969, the temple's "Program of Activities" booklet featured a rendering of the planned new temple on Northeast 122nd Street, while a 1970 photo shows Rabbi Dr. Joseph Gorfinkle with a group of confirmation students at the West Dixie location. The move to the new school was still two years in the future. *Both photos courtesy Temple Beth Moshe.*

There are few rabbis as kind, compassionate, caring, insightful and thoughtful as Rabbi Jory Lang of Temple Beth Moshe, shown here with daughter Sarah at a temple function.

From left are Temple Beth Moshe executive director Marilyn Muravchick Mandel, husband Marvin Mandel and Dr. Merritt D. and Ellen Halem, chairman of the Olympic Village for Special Olympics. Mrs. Mandel, preparing for a well-deserved retirement, has been an absolute dynamo for and on behalf of Beth Moshe. *Both photos courtesy Temple Beth Moshe.*

This page: Temple Beth Sholom on Miami Beach, founded in 1948, has been blessed with two nearly legendary religious leaders. Rabbi Leon Kronish is shown with Israeli writer Elie Wiesel while his successor, Rabbi Gary Glickstein, is shown with his wife, Joanie. *Courtesy Temple Beth Sholom.*

This page: On November 24, 1965, ground was broken for the Morris Lapidus–designed Temple Judea. Almost eight months later, another view from almost the same location on July 16, 1966, shows the progress.

Above: One of the smaller Greater Miami temples was Tifereth Jacob in Hialeah, which was built through and with the assistance of Leo and Ella Galvan. Shown here, Rabbi Leo Heim is holding the Torah presented to the temple by Ella's parents, Yetta and Leo Galvan, at right. At far left is Nate Becker; the names of the two other two men are unknown. *Courtesy Ella Galvan.*

Left: Temple Tifereth Jacob's 1963 Year Book was published to honor the Galvans, shown on the cover, on their twenty-fifth wedding anniversary. Unfortunately, with changing times and demographics, the building was sold in the late 1990s and the temple moved to Miami Lakes, where Rabbi Marvin Rose now presides. *Courtesy Ella Galvan.*

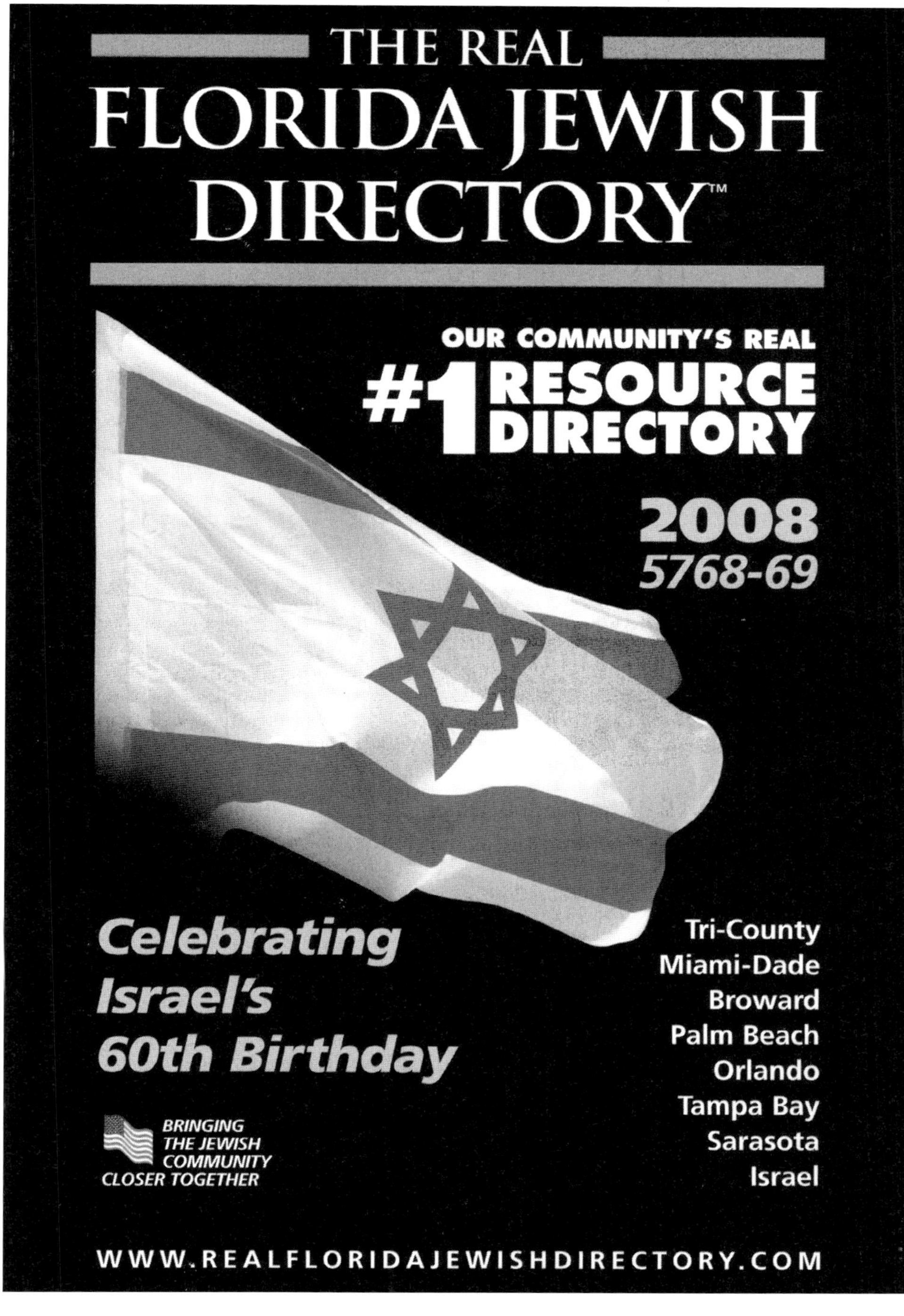

Sandie Morrison has, for the last several years, published *The Real Florida Jewish Directory*; the 2008 edition is shown here. Its 216 pages contain anything and everything that anybody would ever want or need to know about Jewish life in Florida, including complete listings of temples and congregations in much of the state. The listings for the temples, synagogues and chabads in Miami-Dade County are shown on these pages. *Courtesy Sandie Morrison.*

SYNAGOGUES

CONSERVATIVE (C) ORTHODOX (O) REFORM (R) RECONSTRUCTIONIST (REC) UNAFFILIATED (U)

AVENTURA

AVENTURA CHABAD (O)
21001 Biscayne Blvd.
Aventura, FL 33180
(305) 933-0770
Fax: (305) 933-0165
Rabbis: Casriel Brusowankin, Lavi Forta

AVENTURA TURNBERRY JEWISH CENTER– BETH JACOB (C)
20400 NE 30th Ave.
Aventura, FL 33180
(305) 935-0666
Fax: (305) 931-2233
Rabbi: Jonathan Berkun

BEIT DAVID HIGHLAND LAKES SHUL (O)
2601 NE 205th Street
Aventura, FL 33180
(305) 935-4140
Fax: (305) 935-4155
Rabbi: Moshe Rothchild

NER YITZCHOK OF HIGHLAND LAKES AND AVENTURA (O)
2655 NE 207th Street
Aventura, FL 33180
(305) 466-9219
Rabbi: Asher Amselem

WILLIAMS ISLAND SYNAGOGUE (O)
2000 Island Blvd.
Aventura, FL 33160
(305) 936-1288
Fax: (305) 466-3570

COCONUT GROVE

CHABAD OF THE GROVE (O)
3713 Main Highway
Coconut Grove, FL 33133
(305) 445-5444
Fax: (305) 445-5264
Rabbi: Yakov Fellig

CORAL GABLES

TEMPLE JUDEA (R)
5500 Granada Blvd.
Coral Gables, FL 33146
(305) 667-5657
Fax: (305) 665-5834
Rabbi: Edwin Goldberg

HOMESTEAD

TEMPLE HATIKVAH (R)
183 NE 8th St.
Homestead, FL 33030
(305) 248-5724
Fax: (305) 246-3304
Rabbi: Greg Kanter

MIAMI

AHAVAT OLAM (REC)
9085 SW 87th Ave., Suite 210
Miami, FL 33176
(305) 412-4240
Fax: (305) 412-4249
Rabbi: Daniel Marmorstein

BET SHIRA CONGREGATION (C)
7500 SW 120 Street
Miami, FL 33156
(305) 238-2601
Fax: (305) 238-5706
Rabbi: Micah Caplan

BETH DAVID CONGREGATION (C)
2625 SW Third Ave.
Miami, FL 33129
(305) 854-3911
Fax: (305) 285-5841
Rabbi: Hector Epelbaum

B'NAI ISRAEL & GREATER MIAMI YOUTH SYNAGOGUE (O)
16260 SW 288th St.
Miami, FL 33033
(305) 264-6488
Fax: (305) 269-8780

CHABAD CENTER KENDALL (O)
8700 SW 112 St.
Miami, FL 33176
(305) 234-5654
Fax: (305) 278-1903
Rabbi: Yosef Harlig

CONGREGATION BET BREIRA (R)
9400 SW 87th Ave.
Miami, FL 33176
(305) 595-1500
Fax: (305) 279-4147
Rabbi: Jaime Aklepi

TEMPLE BETH AM (R)
5950 N. Kendall Dr.
Miami, FL 33156
(305) 667-6667
Fax: (305) 662-8619
Rabbis: Terry Bookman, James Simon

TEMPLE BETH OR (REC)
11715 SW 87th Ave.
Miami, FL 33176
(305) 235-1419
Fax: (305) 251-8262
Rabbi: Rebecca Lillian

TEMPLE BETH TOV– AHAVAT SHALOM (C)
6438 S.W. 8th Street
Miami, FL 33144
(305) 261-9821
Fax: (305) 279-2845
Rabbi: Manuel Armon

TEMPLE ISRAEL OF GREATER MIAMI (R)
137 N.E. 19 Street
Miami, FL 33132
(305) 573-5900
Fax: (305) 573-5904
Rabbi: Jody Cohen

TEMPLE SAMU-EL OR OLOM (C)
10680 SW 113 Place
Miami, FL 33176
(305) 271-5756
Fax: (305) 271-9660
Rabbi: David Schonblum

TEMPLE ZION ISRAELITE CENTER (C)
3041 NW 7th Street
Miami, FL 33125
(305) 271-2311
Fax: (305) 649-3501
Rabbi: Seymour Friedman

YOUNG ISRAEL OF KENDALL (O)
7880 SW 112 Street
Miami, FL 33156
(305) 232-6833
Fax: (305) 232-6418
Rabbi: Hershel Becker

MIAMI BEACH

ALL PEOPLES SYNAGOGUE (R)
7455 Collins Ave., Suite 201
Miami Beach, FL 33141
(305) 861-5554
Fax: (954) 422-1896
Rabbi: Loring Frank

BETH-EL CONGREGATION (O)
2400 Pine Tree Drive
Miami Beach, FL 33140
(305) 532-6421
Fax: (305) 672-6191

BETH ISRAEL CONGREGATION (O)
770 W. 40th Street
Miami Beach, FL 33140
(305) 538-1251
Fax: (305) 532-0161
Rabbi: Neal Turk

CONGREGATION LUBAVITCH (O)
(AKA Russian Education & Aid Program)
1423 Lenox Ave.
Miami Beach, FL 33139
(305) 673-5493
Fax: (305) 531-7885
Rabbi: Sholom Blank

CONGREGATION OHR CHAIM (O)
317 W. 47th Street
Miami Beach, FL 33140
(305) 674-1326
Fax: (305) 672-7670
Rabbi: Akiva Stolper

SEPHARDIC CONGREGATION OF FLORIDA – TEMPLE MOSES (O)
1200 Normandy Drive
Miami Beach, FL 33141
(305) 861-6308
Fax: (305) 868-6124
Rabbi: Joseph Benchimol

SYNAGOGUES

CONSERVATIVE (C) ORTHODOX (O) REFORM (R) RECONSTRUCTIONIST (REC) UNAFFILIATED (U)

SHAARE EZRA SEPHARDIC CONGREGATION (O)
945 41st Street
Miami Beach, FL 33140
(305) 674-6690
Fax: (305) 674-6691
Rabbi: Yosef Galimidi

SYNAGOGUE OF CARRIAGE CLUB SOUTH (O)
5001 Collins Ave.
Miami Beach, FL 33140
(305) 864-7440
Rabbi: Abraham Avrech

TEMPLE BETH SHMUEL–CUBAN HEBREW CONG. (C)
1700 Michigan Ave.
Miami Beach, FL 33139
(305) 534-7213
Fax:(305) 534-5143
Rabbi: Mayer Abramowitz

TEMPLE BETH SHOLOM (R)
4144 Chase Ave.
Miami Beach, FL 33140
(305) 538-7231
Fax: (305) 531-5428
Rabbis: Gary Glickstein, Robert Davis

TEMPLE EMANU-EL OF GREATER MIAMI (C)
1701 Washington Ave.
Miami Beach, FL 33139
(305) 538-2503
Fax: (305) 535-3134
Rabbi: Kliel Rose

TEMPLE MENORAH (C)
620 75th Street
Miami Beach, FL 33141
(305) 866-0221
Fax: (305) 866-0710
Rabbi: Eliot Pearlson

THE JEWISH LEARNING CENTER (O)
411 41st Street
Miami Beach, FL 33140
(305) 535-0094
Fax: (305) 535-8003

YESHIVA GEDOLAH OF MIAMI (O)
1140 Alton Road
Miami Beach, FL 33139
(305) 673-5664
Fax: (305) 672-0639

YOUNG ISRAEL OF MIAMI BEACH (O)
4221 Pine Tree Drive
Miami Beach, FL 33140
(305) 538-9462
Fax: (305) 531-9462
Rabbi: Donald Bixon

MIAMI LAKES

N.W. DADE COMMUNITY SYNAGOGUE (O)
16800 N.W. 83rd Place
Miami Lakes, FL 33016
(754) 244-2162
Fax: (305) 653-6790
Rabbi: Mendel Weiss

TEMPLE TIFERETH JACOB (C)
5901 N.W. 151st Street, Suite 100
Miami Lakes, FL 33014
(305) 557-2651
Rabbi: Marvin Rose

NORTH BAY VILLAGE

HARAMBAM CONGREGATION (O)
7800 Hispanola Ave.
North Bay Village, FL 33141
(305) 867-0110
Fax: (305) 865-7272
Rabbi: Amram Amselem

NORTH MIAMI

BETH MOSHE CONGREGATION (C)
2225 NE 121st Street
North Miami, FL 33181
(305) 891-5508
Fax: (305) 893-8163
Rabbi: Jory Lang

CHABAD OF NORTH MIAMI (O)
1948 NE 123rd Street
Suite 101-103
North Miami, FL 33181
(305) 892-1234
Fax: (305) 892-1236
Rabbi: Abrohom Lipscyc

N. MIAMI BEACH

BETH TORAH (C)
Benny Rok Campus
20350 NE 26 Ave.
N. Miami Beach, FL 33180
(305) 932-2829
Fax: (305) 933-6955
Rabbis: Edwin Farber, Mario Rojzman

CALIFORNIA CLUB CHABAD (O)
825 N.E. 205 Terrace
N. Miami Beach, FL 33179
(305) 651-1292
Rabbi: Shloime Halsband

CHABAD CHAYIL (O)
1835 N.E. Miami Gardens Dr.
Suite 359
N. Miami Beach, FL 33179
(305) 770-1919
Rabbi: Moishe Kievman

CONGREGATION OR YAACOV (O)
3479 N.E. 163rd Street
N. Miami Beach, FL 33160
(305) 947-2902
Fax: (305) 940-8755
Rabbi: Asher Suissa

CONGREGATION SHAARAY TEFILAH (O)
971 NE 172nd Street
N. Miami Beach, FL 33162
(305) 651-1562
Fax: (305) 654-1406
Rabbi: Ephraim Shapiro

SEPHARDIC JEWISH CENTER OF NMB – CONG. MAGEN DAVID (O)
17100 N.E. 6th Ave.
N. Miami Beach, FL 33162
(786) 553-5396
Fax: (786) 279-1450
Rabbi: Joseph Benarroch

SKYLAKE SYNAGOGUE (O)
1850 N.E. 183rd Street
N. Miami Beach, FL 33179
(305) 945-8712
Fax: (305) 940-8858
Rabbi: Raphael Rosenberg

TEMPLE SINAI (R)
18801 N.E. 22 Ave.
N. Miami Beach, FL 33180
(305) 932-9010
Fax: (305) 933-2443
Rabbi: Alan Litwak
(See Display Ad Page 120)

THE KABBALAH CENTRE (U)
2725 N.E. 163rd St.
N. Miami Beach, FL 33160
(305) 692-9223
(See Display Ad Page 111)

YOUNG ISRAEL OF GREATER MIAMI (O)
990 N.E. 171 Street
N. Miami Beach, FL 33162
(305) 651-3591
Fax: (305) 651-3601
Rabbi: David Lehrfield

SOUTH MIAMI

HAVURAH OF SOUTH FLORIDA (U)
7800 Red Road, Suite 215 E
South Miami, FL 33143
(305) 666-7349

SUNNY ISLES BEACH

CHABAD LUBAVITCH OF SUNNY ISLES BEACH (O)
17555 Atlantic Blvd.
Sunny Isles Beach, FL 33160
(305) 792-4770
Rabbi: Yisrael Baron

CHABAD OF GOLDEN BEACH (O)
19201 Collins Avenue
Sunny Isles Beach, FL 33160
(305) 705-0773
Fax: (305) 705-0223
Rabbi: Chay Amar

CONGREGATION B'NAI ZION (O)
200 - 178th Street
Sunny Isles Beach, FL 33160
(305) 932-2159
Rabbi: Rafael Muratov

TEMPLE BENARROCH BET RAMBAM (O)
18555 Collins Ave.
Sunny Isles Beach, FL 33160
(305) 466-4677
Fax: (305) 933-8181
Rabbi: Marc Benarroch

YOUNG ISRAEL OF SUNNY ISLES (O)
17395 North Bay Road
Sunny Isles Beach, FL 33160
(305) 935-9095

SURFSIDE

THE SHUL – CHABAD OF BAL HARBOUR (O)
9540 Collins Ave.
Surfside, FL 33154
(305) 868-1411
Fax: (305) 861-2426
Rabbi: Sholom Lipskar

YOUNG ISRAEL OF BAL HARBOR (O)
9592 Harding Ave.
Surfside, FL 33154
(305) 866-0203
Fax: (305) 868-1155
Rabbi: Moshe Gruenstein

Chapter Six

The Restaurants and Clubs

There are a bunch of *fressers* aound here…so where can we get a good *nosh*?! Well, as the expression goes, "*ess, totteleh*—you're too skinny!"

According to Sara Leviten in her paper titled "The History of the Miami Jewish Community/1896–1946," the first kosher restaurant and catering service in Miami was named the Palatial Kosher Restaurant and it was located behind the Everglades Hotel, west of Biscayne Boulevard. Opened in the early 1920s by Sunshine (Sunny) Fagan's family, the restaurant was closed in 1945. Sunny married Arthur Hershbein following World War II and their now fifty-nine-year marriage is still going strong!

It is possible, according to a *Miami Herald* article dated August 17, 1973, that the first of the Jewish-style delis in Greater Miami was the Rosedale, originally opened on Miami Beach by New Yorker David Boris (sometimes spelled "Boras") in the early 1920s. Boris was later joined by David Alper and they moved the restaurant to its longtime location on Northwest Fifth Street in Miami. Although the Miami Jewish community was still relatively small, it was large enough to bring in the crowds.

Eventually everybody who lived or worked in or near downtown ate at Rosedale, and it was totally different from Burdine's tearoom and the other *goyisha* dining spots in the area, where a sandwich was one piece of ham, one piece of cheese and some mayo on white bread, as contrasted to the immense, deli-style sandwiches (on rye, of course, with mustard!) at Rosedale. Boris died in 1937 and Alper eventually sold out to Irvin Gordon and Harold Pont, who operated it until the end, but with Rosedale's closing the great Jewish deli era ended in downtown Miami.

Whether at the highest level of culinary and décor excellence (Lloyd's of the Maison Grande, owned by the late Lloyd Apple, being the supreme example), delis or coffee shops, cafeterias, ethnic or natural foods (Al Goldman's Fu Manchu, Ruth Winer's and Ken Lorber's Here Comes the Sun, as examples), great dining places such as the Embers, the Famous, the Newport and Roney Pubs, Cye Mandel's the Hasta, Jack Goldman's Hickory House, Herb and Art Logins Place for Steak, the Piccadilly Hearth on Decorator's Row or more casual dining spots such as Murray Franklin's 12–17 Steak House and Mitch's Steak Ranch, the Jewish people knew not only how to eat but how to prepare and serve.

Fast food was certainly within the province of the Jewish operators, the two best examples being Bill Singer and his Royal Castle chain and Bernie Paley and his Paley's Big Wheel/Kentucky Fried Chicken stores. But, in reality, there were so many special places either owned by Jewish restaurateurs or serving "Jewish-style" food that the list is nearly endless.

One restaurant, however, must be singled out for it is, simply put, nonpareil in the history of Florida, and that is the Weiss and Sawitz families' fabled Joe's Stone Crabs. There is not now nor will there ever be another Joe's, for that incredible dining emporium is the oldest restaurant in the state. The original business, Joe's, first opened on Biscayne Street at Washington Avenue in 1918. While everything at Joe's is nothing short of great, it is worth noting—without fear of contradiction—that the hashed brown potatoes, the coleslaw, the mustard sauce and the key lime pie are the best in America, and in Florida the words "Eat at Joe's" mean only one thing: dining at one of America's greatest restaurants.

The clubs were also terrific and names such as Clover Club, Alan Gale's Celebrity Club, Copa City, Copacabana, Cotton Club, Mocamba and the Latin Quarter are just a very few of the great entertainment spots that should be noted.

As with each of our chapters, it is simply not possible to list every Jewish-owned or Jewish-style restaurant or club that did or does exist but once again, we believe the memories will come flooding back as you enjoy the images of the places we dined in, entertained in and never failed to enjoy.

Blumenfield's, at 668 Collins Avenue, was one of the earliest kosher restaurants. Seated at right, second table against the wall, is Moishe Poopick, a Blumenfield's regular.

Cocktails

Item	Price
Tomato Juice	.35
Stone Crab	2.00
Fresh Shrimp	1.50
Florida Lobster	1.50
Fresh Fruit Cup	.60

Relishes

Item	Price
Celery and Olives	.75
Mixed Pickles	.35
Sweet Pickles	.35
Dill Pickles	.35
Celery	.40
Queen Olives	.40
Stuffed Celery	.75

Soups

Item	Price
Clam Chowder (Cup or Bowl)	.60

Fresh Seafoods (In Season)

Item	Price
Stone Crabs	4.25
Broiled Live Maine Lobster (2 lbs.)	7.00
Pompano, Garlic Butter	4.00
Pompano	3.75
Florida Lobster	2.50
Fried Florida Lobster	2.75
Florida Lobster—Sauted	3.00
Florida Lobster —Sauted in Garlic Butter	3.25
Fried Shrimp—Tartar Sauce	2.50
Shrimp—Sauted	2.75
Shrimp—Sauted in Garlic Butter	3.00
Shrimp Creole	2.50
Fried Oysters	2.25
Blue Fish	2.50
Yellow Tail	2.50
Fried Frog Legs	3.00
Frog Legs—Sauted	3.25
Frog Legs—Sauted in Garlic Butter	3.50
Spanish Mackerel	2.25
Kingfish	2.25
Snapper	2.75
Snapper—Garlic Butter	3.00
Snapper Fingers	3.00
Fried Scallops	2.50
Scallops—Sauted	2.75
Scallops—Sauted in Garlic Butter	3.00

Steaks-Chops Chicken

Item	Price
Sirloin Steak	5.50
Broiled Lamb Chops	4.00
Veal Cutlet with Tomato Sauce	2.75
Half Spring Chicken, Broiled or Fried	2.25
Chopped Tenderloin	2.50
Calf's Liver and Onions or Bacon	2.50

Potatoes

Item	Price
French Fried	.60
Home Fried	.75
Lyonnaise	.75
New Boiled Potatoes	.40
Fried Sweets	.75
Hashed Brown	.75
Julienne	.60
Cottage Fried	.75
Mashed Potatoes	.40
Baked Potatoes	.60

Salads

Item	Price
Fresh Fruit	2.00
Cottage Cheese and Fruit	1.00
Cottage Cheese	.40
Chef's Salad	.60
Hearts of Lettuce	.60
Cole Slaw and Mayonnaise	.60
Stone Crab	4.50
Florida Lobster	2.50
Fresh Shrimp	3.00
Sliced Combination	1.00
Sliced Tomatoes	.60
Lettuce and Tomatoes	.75
Sliced Tomatoes and Onions	.75
Sliced Tomatoes and Cucumbers	.75
Sliced Cucumbers and Onions	.60
Sliced Onions	.40
Sliced Cucumber	.40

Sauces and Dressings

Item	Price
Garlic Sauce	.40
Thousand Island	.40
Russian	.40
Sour Cream	.40
Roquefort	.60
French	
Oil and Vinegar	

Vegetables

Item	Price
Stewed Tomatoes	.60
Garden Spinach	.50
Creamed Garlic Spinach	.75
String Beans	.50
Green Peas	.50
Lima Beans	.50
Broccoli	.75
Green Asparagus	.75
Smothered Onions	.50
French Fried Onions	.75
French Fried Eggplant	.75
Grilled Tomatoes	.75

Desserts

Item	Price
Home Made Apple Pie	.60
Ice Cream	.40
Sherbet	.40
Pie a la Mode	.85
Parfaits	.75
Frozen Eclairs	.75
Strawberry Sundae	.60
Chocolate Sundae	60
Fresh Fruit Cup	.60
Grapefruit	.50
Melon in season	.50

Cheese Saltines

Item	Price
Roquefort	.75
Camembert	.50
Liederkranz	.50
Cheddar	.50

Coffee-Tea Beverages

Item	Price
Coffee (Pot)	.35
Sanka	.35
Tea	.35
Milk	.25
Irish Coffee	1.50

STONE CRABS MAY BE SHIPPED (when available).

All Food Cooked to Order. Please Allow Time for Proper Preparation.

Please order with care. Each item is prepared to your individual order, therefore no substitutions or exchanges can be made.

This and next page: Joe's Stone Crabs is part reality, part legend, and the reality part includes the best food and best service in all of Greater Miami if not in the entire state, far eclipsing hugely overrated eateries such as two in Tampa. Family-owned since day one, the restaurant and its takeaway operation are now superbly managed by Cornell Hotel School graduate Steve Saywitz, great-grandson of Joe, grandson of Jesse and son of Joanne (Weiss) Bass. This 1964–65 season menu indicates that stone crabs were $4.25 for the order, compared to about $40.00 today. The menu itself is a revelation and an indication that, while the prices are different, the food and service aren't: they have stayed great, for in a great restaurant everything is great and there is no "you didn't order the right thing" nonsense. Key lime pie, today's *de rigeur* dessert, was not even on the menu then, and apple pie was $0.60. Indeed, price-wise, those were the days!

JOE'S

Mendelsohn's, at 1301 Collins Avenue, made certain that prospective diners knew it was a kosher establishment.

Al's Sandwich Shop (Al Nemets) at 238 Twenty-third Street was right in the heart of the Miami Beach "tenderloin" district of the late 1930s, '40s and early '50s.

Owned by Dave Taub, this view of the Governor Cafeteria, at 1225 Washington Avenue, will bring back warm memories to anyone who ever enjoyed its ambience.

Park Avenue was at the corner of Twenty-second Street and Park. Suffice to say, it was a great meeting, drinking and dining spot.

This page: Ruth Schwartz's Mocamba Club was one of a kind and was, for its time, one of Greater Miami's hottest spots. Lou Walters's Latin Quarter was one of the first Miami clubs to feature high-grade, elegant, semi-nude show girls, with fine dining an added enhancement.

Above: Sherry-Normandie, on Normandy Isle, later became the kosher Michel's-Normandie but has since gone through a series of owners.

Right: Standing behind the counter inside Raphil's, which was opened on Forty-first Street on Miami Beach in 1948 by Ray Malschick and Phil Seldin, is co-owner Ray Malschick *Courtesy Dr. Judy Malschick.*

Embers host/maitre d' was suave and debonair Mario Talucci, at center. Seated with Mario, who is holding the Embers menu, are, from left, Ed Lassman, former owner of Wolfies; Xavier Cugat, husband of Abbe Lassman Lane; Abbe; and her mom, Mrs. Lassman. *Courtesy Mario Talucci.*

EVERY ONCE IN A WHILE A FAMOUS RESTAURANT IS BORN . . .
WE WERE BORN IN 1945

THE Famous RESTAURANT

OUR FAMOUS
COMPLETE DINNERS INCLUDE:
Choice of Appetizer, Soup, Entree,
Dessert, Hot or Iced Tea,
Hot or Iced Coffee

Fruit Cup
Gefilte Fish
Chilled Pitcha
Stuffed Derma
Sliced Brains
Chopped Liver
Chopped Herring
Schmaltz Herring
Half Grapefruit (in season)
Tomato or Grapefruit Juice
Chopped Roumanian Eggplant
Filet of Pickled Herring in Cream Sauce
Chicken Giblets with Midget Meat Balls
Bill Jordon's Pickled Herring (when available)
Stuffed Cabbage 1.50 extra with any dinner.

Soups

Soup du Jour
Chicken Consomme with Kreplach
or Matzo Ball or Noodles
or Kasha or Rice
Cold Borscht with Sour Cream

Glass of
DOMESTIC WINE
1.25

INQUIRE ABOUT OUR BANQUET FACILITIES

Spanish Menu Available
Menu en Espanol Disponible.

The Famous, at 671 Washington Avenue, was always a treat. The front of the menu is shown here.

Opened on March 15, 1972, Lloyd's of the Maison Grande was operated by Lloyd Apple, who had been the caterer at Temple Beth David and later became food director at Miami Shores Country Club. To this day, Lloyd's remains the most stunningly beautiful restaurant that Greater Miami has ever seen, boasting the table setting that won the *Hospitality Magazine* "Top of the Table" award for finest décor and table setting in America, shown here.

The interior of Fu Manchu, owned by Al Goldman.

Alan Gale's Celebrity Club at Twenty-second Street and Collins Avenue.

Above: At one time, Lincoln and Collins on Miami Beach was a superb business location and Wolfies No. 1 anchored the northeast corner for many years.

Right: Wolfies's 21 was on the corner of Twenty-first Street and Collins Avenue and was, for years, a great rendezvous.

This and opposite page: Concord Cafeteria, at 2021 Collins Avenue, closed in the late 1970s and was the last of Miami's great Jewish-style cafeterias. Holiday Sandwich Shop, on the corner of Twentieth Street and Collins Avenue, had closed some years earlier. Joe Hart's Pickin' Chicken had stores on Twenty-second Street east of Collins Avenue (shown here), at Seventy-first Street and Collins Avenue and at Ninety-first Street and Biscayne Boulevard. The last location noted closed quite early, and its site is now a Publix Market.

TOWN HOUSE HOTEL
Holiday
SANDWICH SHOP
Holiday
RESTAURANT

This page: Bob and Eddie Feinstein opened Mammy's at Sixty-seventh Street and Collins Avenue, the interior shown here. After it was sold to Charlie Linksman and the Bookbinder family in the early 1950s, the name was changed to Pumpernik's. The front of the store, including the pantry/bake shop, is shown here.

This page: As Twenty-third Street on the beach faded, Seventy-ninth Street Causeway in North Bay Village became the new dine, dance and entertainment area, with a wide range of food, beverage and nightclub operations. Betty and Sid Mass's Luau was Polynesian-themed, while the interior of Place for Steak, shown here, was sold by Herb and Art Login to Gil Singer and Boris Pricher, who later sold it to the late Hy Uchitel.

This page: Bagels and Company, David Cohen's terrific deli at 11064 Biscayne Boulevard, along with Michael's New York's Big Apple Deli at 144th and Biscayne, have become the true "in spots" for deli-style breakfast and lunch throughout most of northeast Miami-Dade. Big Apple remains open for dinner, except on Saturday and Sunday nights.

This page: Wilfred E. Cohen came to Miami Beach from Jacksonville, where he had been a partner in Leb's, for many years "the" deli in that city and in Atlanta. Working with several people, including Bill Sherman (Fan and Bill's) and Jerry Cohen, to open a deli-style restaurant at Twenty-first Street and Collins Avenue, they held a contest to come up with a name for the store. The contest was won by a University of Miami student and the name selected was Wolfie's. Shortly thereafter, Wilfred E. Cohen legally changed his first name, and the rest, as they say, was history. The interior of his Rascal House is shown here in 1954; a later advertising postcard is also pictured.

Arthur Horowitz built his name and fame with a great group of four restaurants in Miami Beach, Sunny Isles, Coral Gables and on the corner of Seventy-ninth Street and Biscayne Boulevard in Miami; that eatery is shown here on November 24, 1966.

The Singer family's Royal Castle was "everywhere," and for hamburgers, birch beer or breakfast, "RC" was the place. This store, pictured on May 22, 1961, was located at the corner of Northwest First Street and First Avenue, just across from the Dade County Courthouse.

Above: Bernie Paley, whose brother, Seymour, owned and operated Corky's Deli and Sandwich Shop on Northeast 163rd Street in North Miami Beach was famous for his Paley's Big Wheel and Kentucky Fried Chicken chain. The store at 2590 Biscayne Boulevard is shown here.

Right: For beautiful showgirls, great shows, superb food and a wonderful host, Jack Goldman's Clover Club on Biscayne Boulevard in downtown Miami was, as the back of this circa 1953 menu states, "Miami's Number One Supper Club," with prices, at the time, to match. Complete dinners ranged from \$4.50 to \$8.00; whole broiled lobster was \$4.95 and a double rack of lamb chops was \$6.50. But even then…it was worth it!

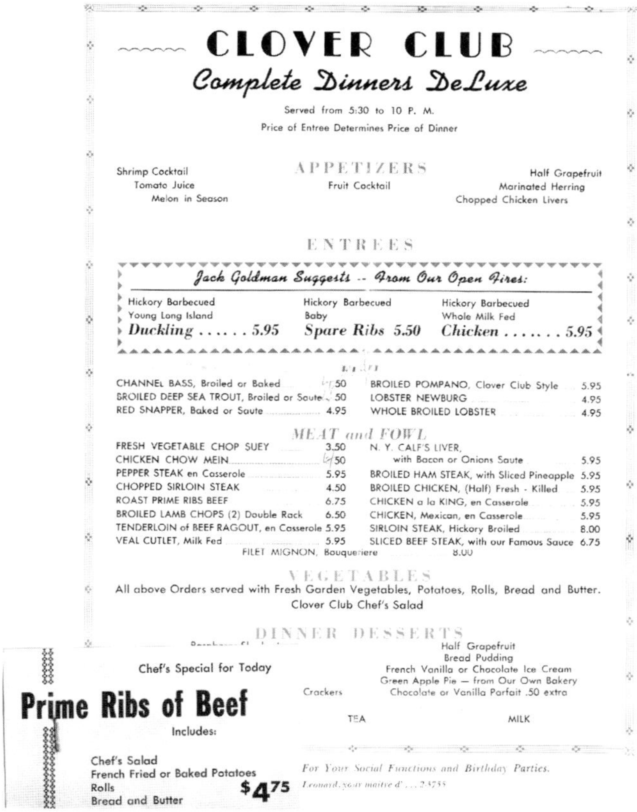

CLOVER CLUB

Complete Dinners DeLuxe

Served from 5:30 to 10 P. M.
Price of Entree Determines Price of Dinner

APPETIZERS

Shrimp Cocktail
Tomato Juice
Melon in Season
Fruit Cocktail
Half Grapefruit
Marinated Herring
Chopped Chicken Livers

ENTREES

Jack Goldman Suggests -- From Our Open Fires:

Hickory Barbecued Young Long Island **Duckling 5.95**
Hickory Barbecued Baby **Spare Ribs 5.50**
Hickory Barbecued Whole Milk Fed **Chicken 5.95**

CHANNEL BASS, Broiled or Baked 4.50
BROILED DEEP SEA TROUT, Broiled or Saute 4.50
RED SNAPPER, Baked or Saute 4.95
BROILED POMPANO, Clover Club Style 5.95
LOBSTER NEWBURG 4.95
WHOLE BROILED LOBSTER 4.95

MEAT and FOWL

FRESH VEGETABLE CHOP SUEY 3.50
CHICKEN CHOW MEIN 6.50
PEPPER STEAK en Casserole 5.95
CHOPPED SIRLOIN STEAK 4.50
ROAST PRIME RIBS BEEF 6.75
BROILED LAMB CHOPS (2) Double Rack 6.50
TENDERLOIN of BEEF RAGOUT, en Casserole 5.95
VEAL CUTLET, Milk Fed 5.95
N. Y. CALF'S LIVER, with Bacon or Onions Saute 5.95
BROILED HAM STEAK, with Sliced Pineapple 5.95
BROILED CHICKEN, (Half) Fresh - Killed 5.95
CHICKEN a la KING, en Casserole 5.95
CHICKEN, Mexican, en Casserole 5.95
SIRLOIN STEAK, Hickory Broiled 8.00
SLICED BEEF STEAK, with our Famous Sauce 6.75
FILET MIGNON, Bouquetiere 8.00

VEGETABLES

All above Orders served with Fresh Garden Vegetables, Potatoes, Rolls, Bread and Butter.
Clover Club Chef's Salad

DINNER DESSERTS

Half Grapefruit
Bread Pudding
French Vanilla or Chocolate Ice Cream
Green Apple Pie — from Our Own Bakery
Crackers
Chocolate or Vanilla Parfait .50 extra

TEA
MILK

Chef's Special for Today

Prime Ribs of Beef

Includes:

Chef's Salad
French Fried or Baked Potatoes
Rolls
Bread and Butter

\$4.75

For Your Social Functions and Birthday Parties.

Chapter Seven

The Hotels—And Two That Became a Hospital

There is, it appears, some dispute over which hotel was the first Jewish-owned hostelry in Greater Miami. While the chronicling of the restaurants appears to be if not completely thorough then at least relatively accurate, the pinpointing of an opening date for the first Jewish-owned hotel seems to be clouded in the mists of time.

One thing is certain, however, and that is the fact that the first Jewish-owned hotel on Miami Beach was the Nemo, which opened in 1921 at First Street and Collins Avenue. Owned by New Englander Sam Magid (Myra Farr's mother's brother and her favorite uncle) and built and operated by Joseph and Harry Goodkowsky (the latter was Myra's father), who had owned and managed the famous and popular (and kosher) Lafayette Hotel in Old Orchard Beach, Maine, the hotel was the first in Miami Beach to cater to those whose dietary preference was kosher. The Seabreeze at Second and Collins, which also followed dietary laws, opened shortly thereafter.

Sometime in the mid-1920s, the Jacobs family opened the first of three hotels, and the family name has been prominent in the hospitality business on Miami Beach since that time. In 1926, the three-story (St.) David Court opened at 56 Washington Avenue and it was that apartment-hotel in which religious services—the first on Miami Beach for the Jewish community—were held.

A number of Jewish hoteliers began to either purchase or build new facilities. In 1929, Nathan Stone, the grandfather of Florida's future U.S. Senator Richard Stone, opened the multistory Blackstone Hotel at Eighth Street and Washington Avenue, while the Nash family bought the William Penn, a couple of blocks south, making the name "Nash" a prefix to the former name. A number of smaller, Jewish-owned hotels opened throughout the 1930s, the art deco building boom a prewar prelude to what would follow. Names such as Henry Hohauser, the great architect, became familiar to anybody coming to Miami with a desire to invest and to build.

Following World War II, a different breed of Jewish hotelman emerged, with dreams of grandeur for the Miami area far greater than anybody could have previously imagined. Within a short time many of the motels and hotels in Sunny Isles, Miami Beach and on Biscayne Boulevard were built and owned by people of the Jewish faith.

Among the names that resound in Greater Miami hotel history are the two different Kipnis families, the Rose and Unger families, Jerry Sussman, Jerry Olin, Dave Levinson, Stirling Levine, Ted Hankoff, Sam Cohen, Morris Lansburgh, Harry Mufson, Sherman Winn, Harry Singer, Ben Novack, Irving Pollack, "Red" Pollack, Al Pollack, Jack Parker, Larry Paskow, George Sax, Julius and Ben Gaines, the brothers Kaskel and a good few more.

In the early to mid-1950s, Norman Giller and Morris Lapidus reached new heights in architecture and design as they created fanciful new buildings, bringing the public the numerous unique motels in Sunny Isles and great new hotels, including the Fontainebleau and the Eden Roc, on Miami Beach.

In Dade County's history, two hospitals, now operated as one, emerged from restricted clientele hotels. Mount Sinai Hospital was originally the Nautilus Hotel at Forty-fourth Street and Alton Road. Miami Heart Institute (the former King Cole Hotel) on Forty-eighth Street east of Alton Road was not a Jewish institution at the time; its original founders and benefactors were, for the most part, gentile.

With changing demographics, however, and the vicissitudes of time supposedly rendering the need for two major healthcare facilities within Miami Beach redundant (at least according to Mount Sinai's management), Mount Sinai purchased Miami Heart, the latter now for sale and a restriction on the sale (the word "restriction" relating to a sale still distasteful, even these many years later) that the land must be used, according to published reports, for something other than a healthcare facility of any kind. This sounds awfully close to an agreement, if made, that is in restraint of trade, for if it is allowed to happen Mount Sinai will be the only hospital remaining of the four that once existed on the entire east side of Biscayne Bay, from Government Cut on the south to the county line on the north.

As with the previous chapters, the reader is asked to recognize that it is not possible to list every Jewish-owned hotel or motel or to list the names of every person of the faith who owned a hotel or motel. Rather, as with the preceding chapters, the goal is to present to the reader a panorama of images portraying the various kinds, types and styles of the Jewish-owned or -managed properties.

So let the bellhop take you to your room and then sit back, relax and allow the memories to come flooding through as you enjoy reading and reminiscing about those happy—if not glorious—days and weeks that you spent staying, dining, meeting new people at, having a drink or working in the hotels owned by our Jewish friends and neighbors.

Jewish businesspeople operated apartment houses as well as hotels. The Mayfair Apartments were on Park or Liberty Avenues near what would become the area of the Miami Beach Convention Center. Shown in the picture is Harry Trachman, who was staying at the Mayfair before buying his home on the corner of Twenty-third Street and Meridian Avenue. *Courtesy Yetta Brodie.*

This page: The President Apartments were at 301 Collins Avenue, and the Mecca at 245 Collins. *Both photos courtesy Quentin Sandler.*

This page: The Mantell Plaza, owned by John Mantell, was on the west side of Lake Pancoast, occupying the land between Flamingo and Lake Pancoast Drives. *Courtesy Gloria Pallot.*

This and opposite page: Now a retirement home, the Blackstone was, for many years, a prominent Jewish-owned hostelry, as was the William Penn after the Nash family bought it. Faber's Park Apartment Hotel offered very attractive weekly rates, even at the height of "the season" in the late 1950s and early 1960s.

Where Friends Meet Friends

FABER'S

Park Apartment Hotel

928 Ocean Drive Miami Beach 39, Florida

Telephone JE 8-4726

WEEKLY RATES FOR HOTEL ROOMS

From May to Nov.	**$15.00 to $25.00**
November	**15.00 to 25.00**
December	**30.00 to 40.00**
January	**40.00 to 50.00**
February	**60.00 to 70.00**
March	**40.00 to 50.00**
April	**25.00 to 35.00**

These rates are for two persons in the hotel rooms. A 10% charge for each additional person.

All Rooms are Air Conditioned

Air-conditioned rooms and apartments individually controlled.

Free Parking for Your Car On Our Parking Lot.

Over

A close-up of the Castaways addition on the west side of Collins Avenue. The famous Wreck Bar was in this building.

SWEET SIXTEEN LUNCHEON

honoring

REGINA VICTORIA PERLMUTTER

Saturday, January 9, 1960 — Scheherazade Room

REGINA VICTORIA PERLMUTTER

hotel Algiers

Oceanfront, 25th to 26th Street, Miami Beach, Florida

Menu

Supreme of Fresh Fruit
au Mint

SOUTHERN FRIED CHICKEN MARYLAND

Glazed Sweet Potato — New Garden Peas

Luncheon Rolls

Tossed Green Salad
French Dressing

PARFAIT REGINA
Sweet Sixteen Cake

Coffee

A beguiling Regina (Reggie) Perlmutter celebrated her sweet sixteen with a luncheon at the Scheherazade Room of the Dave Levinson–owned Algiers Hotel at Twenty-fifth Street and Collins Avenue. *Courtesy Regina Goldstein.*

The Stirling Levine–owned Montmartre was a delightfully informal property, one of the last hotels built on Miami Beach between the late 1960s and the 1990s.

The Lucerne, at Forty-first Street and Collins Avenue, just north of the Crown, was, for a good few years, another popular hotel.

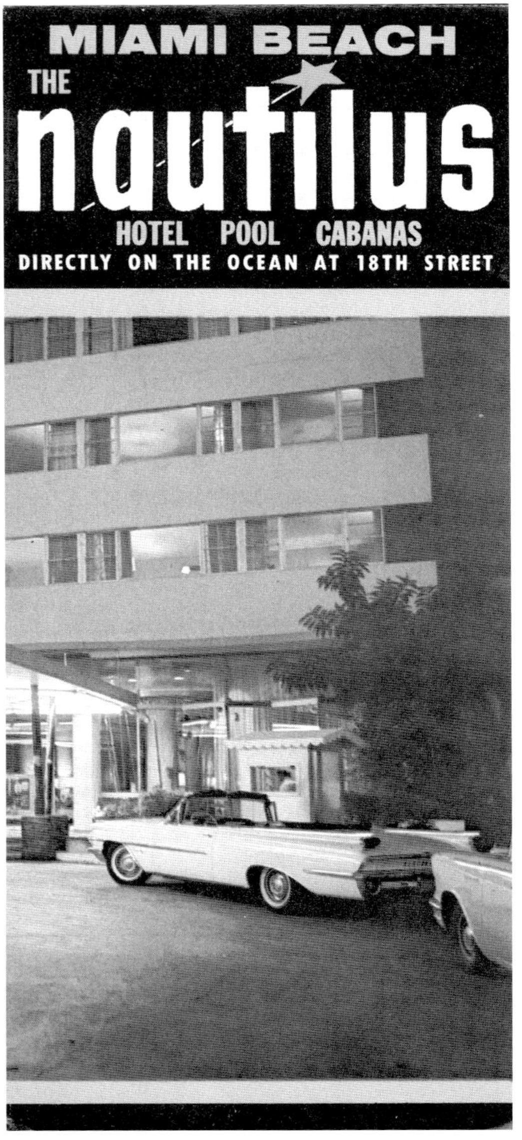

Irving Pollack's Nautilus (built long after the original hotel of the same name became a hospital), at Eighteenth Street and Collins Avenue, is shown here.

Sam Cohen's Deauville replaced the old McFadden-Deauville on the same site. Built in 1957–58, the hotel is still an active Miami Beach hostelry, although long out of Cohen ownership.

Hortense Landesman Arvan and Rosalind Klein, both Bergida descendants, stand under the David Court sign at 56 Washington Avenue in 1930. *Courtesy Dr. Arlene Amarant.*

Robert Richter was a Jewish boy shot down over Germany in World War II. To honor his memory, the Richter family purchased the former Whitman Hotel and named it for their son. An early 1950s summer promotional flyer is shown here.

Above: The beautiful Eden Roc Hotel, just north of the Fontainebleau, opened in 1955.

Right: The Fontainebleau took the title of Miami Beach's flagship hotel from the Roney Plaza. In one of the most despicable actions ever engaged in on Miami Beach, the late Ben Novack, who built and owned the Fontainebleau at the time, had the Towers building constructed with its north wall—which faced the Eden Roc's pool area—completely devoid of both windows and paint. It is for that, more than for anything else that he was known to have done, that Novack will be most remembered.

Left: Owned by the Rose and Unger families, the Royal Palm, on Collins Avenue between Fifteenth and Sixteenth Streets, offered special summer rates in the late 1940s.

Below: The two Carl Fisher hotels that would become hospitals were the Nautilus and the King Cole; a photograph of the latter is shown here.

This booklet may be the only copy that exists of this 1924 opening season promotional for the Nautilus Hotel. Following the hotel's use as an army hospital during World War II, a "temporary citizen's committee of the Jewish hospital" of five people was formed. On March 11, 1946, the temporary committee enlarged itself to seventeen members and incorporated as Mount Sinai Hospital of Greater Miami, Inc. The purchase of the fifty-five-bed Alton Road Hospital, then located at Seventh and Alton (the later site of the now closed South Shore Hospital), from the City of Miami Beach following World War II would eventually lead the way to the turning over of the Nautilus property to the City of Miami Beach, which, through a quitclaim deed, transferred the property to the Mount Sinai group. The Alton Road property was then sold and the new Mount Sinai Hospital, the former Nautilus Hotel, opened on Sunday, December 4, 1949, under the management of executive director Samuel Gertner, who remained in that position until his death in 1974.

Chapter Eight

THE GREATER MIAMI JEWISH FEDERATION

If there is any organization that has led the way in terms of generosity and providing for the Jewish people of South Florida, it has been the Greater Miami Jewish Federation. Founded in 1938 in response to Kristallnacht (considered the start of the Holocaust), the Federation has worked to build our community for more than seventy years. The man credited with starting the Federation, with working so incredibly hard to bring the various disparate Jewish groups together, is Stanley C. Myers, for whom the Federation's building at 4200 Biscayne Boulevard is named.

The Federation, through its network of beneficiary agencies and services, provides humanitarian needs to people of all ages. The organization helps those in need of food, housing, transportation, counseling, socialization and more, all in a Jewish setting, and the Federation is the forefront of creating and supporting programs for youth that help strengthen Jewish identity and pride.

A listing of organizations that benefit from the Federation's programs would take, literally, pages. It is, however, important to note that there are numerous and various agencies, services and departments within the Federation that serve so many, both individuals and organizations, in Miami and in Israel, providing a vast array of support services and assistance to Jewish people in need and managing a variety of programs and activities that are designed to serve the Jewish community in the areas of campaign, community education, leadership development, community services, human resources outreach and synagogue, agency and Federation relations.

Suffice to say, the leadership of the Federation, from Mr. Myers's founding of the organization in 1938, has been extraordinary. Today, under the guidance and direction of Executive Vice-president Jacob Solomon and current President Saby Behar (William Lehman Jr. is president-elect) and with the support of a dedicated and diverse board of directors, the Federation continues to be the principal and guiding agency of and for Jewish causes and concerns, as well as for Jewish welfare and well-being in Greater Miami and much of south Florida.

Unless otherwise credited, all photographs in this chapter are courtesy of the Greater Miami Jewish Federation.

Left: From left, Sam Blank, founding President Stanley C. Myers, Herb Scher, Jake Sher and Carl Weinkle at a Federation meeting, early 1940s.

Below: Sometime in the 1940s, members of the Jewish community welcomed Harry S. Truman to Miami on behalf of the Federation/Combined Jewish Appeal campaign.

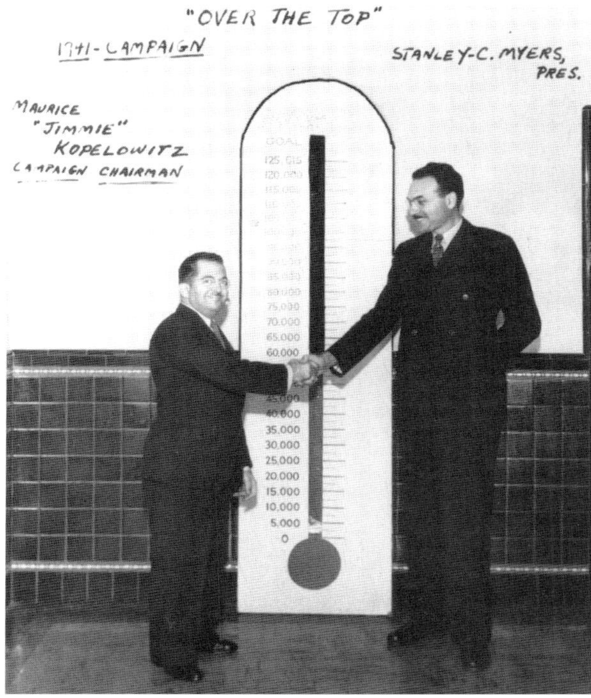

Maurice "Jimmie" Kopelowitz (campaign chairman) and founding president Stanley C. Myers are delighted as the Federation fundraising campaign for 1941 reaches the goal of nearly $126,000.

Federation News

PUBLISHED BY THE GREATER MIAMI JEWISH FEDERATION

VOLUME 1, NUMBER 5 — MIAMI, FLORIDA — DECEMBER, 1945

1946 Combined Jewish Appeal of Greater Miami

FEBRUARY 24 - MARCH 6

70 CAUSES . . . ONE APPEAL

MORRIS KLASS RETURNS

Greater Miami Jewish Federation is happy to welcome back from the U. S. Army its Executive Director. Mr. Klass is in the midst of planning the 1946 Campaign.

FEDERATION POLICY ON USE OF MASTER FILE

In response to many requests of organizations for the Federation Master File, Max Orovitz, Chairman of the Executive Committee, announced that a policy has been established by the Executive Committee as follows:

"The Master File of Federation will not be available in the future for the use of any organization or individual outside of Federation itself. However, the Federation office will stand ready to offer a mailing service at cost, to reach all residents on its list provided the material to be mailed receives the approval of the Federation Master File Sub-Committee of which Isaac Levin is Chairman."

This will permit organizations wishing to announce communal affairs the opportunity to reach all Miami residents of the Jewish Faith.

BOARD VOTE TIED

The Council of Jewish Federations and Welfare Funds recommended National Advisory Budgeting to its member agencies, and the Greater Miami Jewish Federation Board of Directors considered the question at the meeting November 15th.

Leading a spirited debate on the question were Mrs. Benjamin Meyers, who presented the affirmative aspects and Mr. I. S. Shapoff, in place of Mrs. S. H. Leslie, the negative.

"National Advisory Budgeting is defined as a review by a national committee selected by the Council or by the welfare fund members of the Council. Where joint decisions could not be reached, the Committee would advise the welfare funds as to the part of the agency's budget and program of work which had been agreed upon and would present both sides of the major items of difference. The Committee would not attempt to establish local quotas."

Several members of the Board participated in this discussion. Stanley C. Myers outlined the history of the project. Mr. Myers was one of the 18 individuals from 10 communities composing the Committee on the Study of National Budgeting Proposals organized in 1940. This Study Committee approached the problem objectively in an earnest effort to find the answer as to whether advisory budgeting service was desirable and necessary. The President of the Greater Miami Jewish Federation, Max Orovitz, then asked Mr. Myers to answer questions which the Board members wished to ask. Mr. Myers concluded by urging the Board to vote the acceptance of National Advisory Budgeting. Rabbi Max Shapiro who was opposed to National Advisory Budgeting explained his reasons for refusing to accept it at this time. The discussion was closed; the Board voted on the question, and the result was a tie vote. A letter will be sent explaining the position of the delegates from Miami and the tie vote.

The United Jewish Appeal has called a meeting of the leaders of American Jewry on December 15th in order that we may truly have the benefit of thorough-going analysis and discussion of what American Jews can and ought to do to help hundreds of thousands of Jews to survive. Delegates representing Greater Miami are Max Orovitz, President; Rabbi Max Shapiro, Chairman of the Budget Committee; William Singer, Chairman of the 1946 Campaign, and Morris Klass, Executive Director of the Greater Miami Jewish Federation.

This year's Federation Campaign is set up on a Trades Division basis. In addition to the usual "special gifts" affair, there will be a number of Trade's Division solicitation meetings. These meetings are very desirable from a standpoint of conserving time and effort consumed in making individual solicitations.

William Singer, Chairman, stated: "There will be no pressure methods used in any solicitation this year, and we urge you to cooperate."

William D. Singer

William D. Singer, Chairman of the 1946 Campaign, is a vice-President of Federation and has served on the Budget and Executive Committees in past years. Mr. Singer will announce his committees in the next issue of the Federation News.

PICTURE OF YOUR BUDGET COMMITTEE AT WORK
1946 CAMPAIGN
Leon Kaplan, Mrs. Milton Sirkin, Dr. Albert Rosenthal, Mrs. S. H. Leslie, I. Furst, S. Lefcourt, Abraham Goodman, H. Cornblum, Rabbi Max Shapiro, Chairman, Morris Klass, Executive Director, Herbert E. Scher, Shepard Broad

In December 1945, the Federation issued volume 1, number 5 of *Federation News*, the cover featuring the fact that although there were seventy causes there was one united appeal for funds. *Courtesy Karen Lytton Levin.*

Above: In honor of the late Stanley C. Myers, founding president, the Greater Miami Jewish Federation Building at 4200 Biscayne Boulevard, Miami, was rededicated in December 1993. Then-president Steven J. Kravitz speaks from the podium as Myers's son, Kenneth Myers, unveils the new name.

Left: Israel's Deputy Consul General Dan Haezrachy, *left*, celebrates Israel's golden anniversary in April 1998 with Miami's Israel 50 Chair Norman Braman, a past president of the Greater Miami Jewish Federation.

From left: Former Israeli Prime Minister Shimon Peres and Federation Vice-president Emeritus Myron J. "Mike" Brodie greet Florida Governor Bob Graham during a 1998 event.

Federation President Michael M. Adler addresses the audience at a 2006 program in Israel celebrating the twenty-fifth anniversary of a partnership between the Jewish communities of Miami and Or Akiva, Israel.

In October 2007, Greater Miami Jewish Federation leadership signed a Covenant of Partnership with representatives of Yerucham, a thirteen-square-mile city in Israel's Negev Region and home to 9,400 residents from many cultural and ethnic backgrounds. *Pictured are*: Ouri Liberti, Yerucham Steering Committee chair; Bobbie Higer, Miami Steering Committee chair; the Honorable Amram Mitzna, Yerucham mayor and retired Israel Defense Forces officer; and (signing Covenant) Federation President Saby Behar.

From left: Greater Miami Jewish Federation President Saby Behar, Morrie Siegel, Lezlie Poyastro, General Campaign Chair William Lehman Jr. and Executive Vice-president Jacob Solomon in Israel during the Federation Solidarity Mission in August 2006.

At the Greater Miami Jewish Federation's main event in January 2008, Executive Vice-president Emeritus Myron J. "Mike" Brodie received the Federation's Friend of Israel Humanitarian Award for his lifetime of service to the Jewish community. *Pictured, left to right*: Federation immediate past President Michael M. Adler; past Presidents Michael Scheck and Ezra Katz; Executive Vice-president Jacob Solomon; past Presidents Steven J. Kravitz, Isaac Zelcer, Norman Lipoff, Harry B. Smith and Nedra Oren; Myron J. "Mike" Brodie; past President Donald E. Lefton; Federation President Saby Behar; and past Presidents Aaron Podhurst and Harry "Hap" Levy.

Chapter Nine

The Miami Jewish Home and Hospital for the Aged at Douglas Gardens

The story of the founding, growth and incredible contributions to the community made by the Jewish Home are beyond belief, and were they not absolute fact it would be easy to believe that the story of the Home emanates from a novel, for its genesis came from a gentile and the founding of it was instigated by none other than Ida Cohen.

The story of the Miami Jewish Home began with two people: Adam Reiss and Ida Cohen. In 1939, in a gesture of extreme love and caring meant to repay the Jewish community for kindnesses extended years previously, Reiss left $10,000 in trust with Ida for the purpose of establishing a place where elderly persons of the Jewish faith could retire with dignity. In early 1940, Ida called together a group of prominent Jewish citizens to propound the idea of a "Jewish Home."

Opening in 1945 with twenty-three elderly widows and widowers as residents, the Home is today the largest nonprofit geriatric care center in the Southeast, a result of the love, caring and dedication of the original founders and those who would follow. Some of those later supporters would earn, through their generous donations, the honorary designation of "Founder," consecrating the foresight and vision of such legendary Jewish Miami pioneers as Ida and Isidor Cohen, Mr. and Mrs. Daniel Broad, Judge and Mrs. Harold Spaet, Claire and Sydney Weintraub, Baron deHirsch Meyer and others.

Each year, through the continuing care of staff, as well as hundreds of loving members, volunteers and families, close to seven hundred residents of the twenty-acre Douglas Gardens campus, as well as those living at Douglas Gardens North plus thousands more served at and by the Home's off-campus facilities, are the beneficiaries of those who, in the late 1930s and early 1940s, believed in a dream that has made the Miami Jewish Home and Hospital the benchmark in and for world-class healthcare.

As with the Federation, the story of the Home is book length and the work done by the pioneers, the time spent, the dedication, the loving care and above all the belief in the future have made the Home a place filled with love and kindness, with a staff that, once becoming part of the Home's family, generally remains with the Home for years. It is not uncommon for employees to retire with twenty-five or more years of service.

Many of the names familiar to Greater Miami philanthropy are among the Home's benefactors and that list alone would take several pages, including Isabel and Sam May, who dedicated the visitors' center; the Ungar family, who funded the ice cream parlor; Helen Rechtshaffer, who donated the synagogue in the Hazel Cypen Tower; Gus Trau; the Blooms; the Heymanns; the Lifschitzs; the Chernins; the Abels; the deHirsch Meyers; the Rubys; the Becks; the Toppels; the Schaeffers; the Steins; the Ablins; the Harrises; and so very many more who have donated property, built buildings and enabled growth. But perhaps foremost in the Home's history are two names that have become synonymous with the Home: Hazel and Judge Irving Cypen.

A wonderful story is told about Irving Cypen first being invited to join the board of directors, for it was at that meeting that Daniel Broad is alleged to have said, "Who invited the *kinder*?" The *kinder*, happily for the board and the Home, turned out to be a godsend, for it was Irving, with Hazel at his side, who took on the task of building a world-class institution. There are, of course, hundreds if not thousands more, from Founders-level members to volunteers who give willingly of their time in order to continue to maintain the Home at a level that is nonpareil for facilities of its kind.

The Miami Jewish Home and Hospital for the Aged at Douglas Gardens, along with the new Douglas Gardens North Campus in Pembroke Pines, stands alone as the outstanding beacon of hope and home not only for those entering their retirement years but also for those in need of mental and physical rehabilitation. Because of its loving, caring staff, state-of-the-art campuses, marvelously maintained facilities and highest quality of service, the Home is the only four-star ACLF/nursing home/rehab facility in the state of Florida.

Above: The original facility for the initially named Jewish Home for the Aged in Miami, Florida, Inc. opened in 1945, after five years of fundraising and hard work. The building, at 335 Southwest Twelfth Avenue, originally housed twenty-three elderly widows and widowers. That building, with some of its first residents and family members, is shown here.

Right: On June 27, 1940, shortly after the first meeting was held to organize the Home, the minutes of the meeting of that date were forwarded to officers and members; the first page is shown here. Many names that are familiar to the reader and who are Jewish Miami pioneers are visible, both on the left and in the typed list, center.

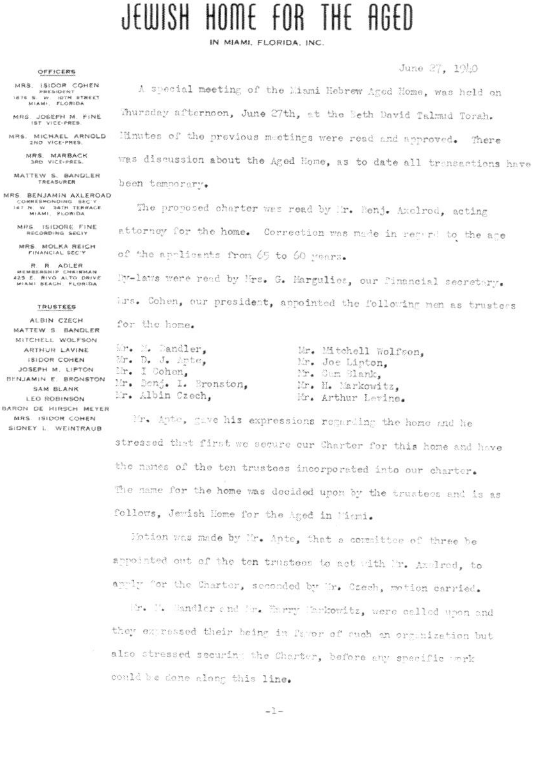

JEWISH HOME FOR THE AGED

IN MIAMI, FLORIDA, INC.

OFFICERS

MRS. ISIDOR COHEN
PRESIDENT
1676 S. W. 10TH STREET
MIAMI, FLORIDA

MRS. JOSEPH M. FINE
1ST VICE-PRES.

MRS. MICHAEL ARNOLD
2ND VICE-PRES.

MRS. MARBACK
3RD VICE-PRES.

MATTEW S. BANDLER
TREASURER

MRS. BENJAMIN AXLEROAD
CORRESPONDING SEC'Y
147 N. W. 34TH TERRACE
MIAMI, FLORIDA

MRS. ISIDORE FINE
RECORDING SEC'Y

MRS. MOLKA REICH
FINANCIAL SEC'Y

R. R. ADLER
MEMBERSHIP CHAIRMAN
425 E. RIVO ALTO DRIVE
MIAMI BEACH, FLORIDA

TRUSTEES

ALBIN CZECH
MATTEW S. BANDLER
MITCHELL WOLFSON
ARTHUR LAVINE
ISIDOR COHEN
JOSEPH M. LIPTON
BENJAMIN E. BRONSTON
SAM BLANK
LEO ROBINSON
BARON DE HIRSCH MEYER
MRS. ISIDOR COHEN
SIDNEY L. WEINTRAUB

June 27, 1940

A special meeting of the Miami Hebrew Aged Home, was held on Thursday afternoon, June 27th, at the Beth David Talmud Torah. Minutes of the previous meetings were read and approved. There was discussion about the Aged Home, as to date all transactions have been temporary.

The proposed charter was read by Mr. Benj. Axelrod, acting attorney for the home. Correction was made in regard to the age of the applicants from 65 to 60 years.

By-laws were read by Mrs. G. Margulies, our financial secretary. Mrs. Cohen, our president, appointed the following men as trustees for the home.

Mr. M. Bandler,
Mr. D. J. Apte,
Mr. I Cohen,
Mr. Benj. I. Bronston,
Mr. Albin Czech,

Mr. Mitchell Wolfson,
Mr. Joe Lipton,
Mr. Sam Blank,
Mr. H. Markowitz,
Mr. Arthur Levine.

Mr. Apte, gave his expressions regarding the home and he stressed that first we secure our Charter for this home and have the names of the ten trustees incorporated into our charter. The name for the home was decided upon by the trustees and is as follows, Jewish Home for the Aged in Miami.

Motion was made by Mr. Apte, that a committee of three be appointed out of the ten trustees to act with Mr. Axelrod, to apply for the Charter, seconded by Mr. Czech, motion carried.

Mr. M. Bandler and Mr. Harry Markowitz, were called upon and they expressed their being in favor of such an organization but also stressed securing the Charter, before any specific work could be done along this line.

-1-

Pioneer Certificate

Mr. and Mrs. Sidney L. Weintraub

were pioneers in founding

THE JEWISH HOME for the AGED
of GREATER MIAMI, FLORIDA

presented on April 11th, 1954 at the Ablin Memorial Ground-Breaking Ceremonies, in appreciation of their leadership and devotion to the Home and in the cause of the Jewish aged~

Abe Kurman
President

M. J. Kopelowitz
Chairman of the Board

This page: At the Ablin Memorial groundbreaking ceremony in 1954, the Home's pioneers—the original members—received their Pioneer Certificates. Sidney and Claire Weintraub's certificate is shown here. At that ceremony, Ida Cohen and Judge Irving Cypen prepare for the ceremonial groundbreaking.

Right: Many of the Home's residents look forward to the care they receive in the beauty salon. In 1996, hairdresser Mirtha Mendez was adjusting the curlers in 1-Chernin resident Marie Acosta's hair.

Below: Although they are now in semi-retirement, Hazel and Judge Irving Cypen will always be memorialized as the couple who led the Home to its current level of greatness. Fortunately for the Home's entire family, the Cypen's son, Stephen, a member of the Florida bar and longtime participant in the Home's affairs and activities, has been named chairman of the board. His father is now chairman of the board emeritus and honorary president. Here, Judge Cypen, with his trademark bowtie, is with Hazel as they welcome former Florida Governor Leroy Collins to the Home. *Both photos courtesy Miami Jewish Home and Hospital.*

Chapter Ten

The Jewish Museum of Florida

Like so much in this book, the story of the genesis and founding of the Jewish Museum of Florida is not just incredible but, like Miami Beach's Art Deco District, the Federation and the Jewish Home, there is one person who was either the founder or the nucleus of growth and development. In the case of the museum, that person is one and the same.

Marcia-Jo Kerstein Zerivitz came from the Orlando area, her interest in Jewish history always being central to her academic being. More than twenty-five years ago she learned that there was almost no documentation of Jewish life in Florida from the earliest years, and that knowledge propelled her to travel ceaselessly around the state to gather material, historic documents and memorabilia chronicling the history of the Jewish people in Florida, beginning with the arrival of the first Jews in 1763.

Begun in 1984 as MOSAIC, the project expanded in 1986 to a statewide effort to document Florida Jewish history. With a grant from the Florida Department of State, a project team was assembled and Marcia traveled to more than thirty cities to conduct research and train hundreds of volunteers to collect family photographs, documents and artifacts and conduct innumerable oral histories. Ultimately, she traveled more than 150,000 miles in pursuit of Florida's Jewish history.

From the early collection, a colorful exhibit was produced by a team consisting of, among others, Marcia, Laura Hochman and Abe Gittelson. Opening in 1990 at the Historical Museum of Southern Florida in Miami, the exhibit traveled to ten other cities within the state through 1993 and then was exhibited nationally.

As the exhibit traveled, enthusiasm mounted for a permanent museum of Jewish history that would continue to collect and preserve that history and that could relate to all ethnic groups. Marcia-Jo Zerivitz was the obvious choice to become founding executive director. In 1992, a board of directors was assembled and a capital campaign was initiated. Eventually, after examining several sites throughout the state, the edifice that had served for so long as Temple Beth Jacob on Miami Beach was selected as the venue for the museum.

The temple, although still minimally active, was in danger of closing and Marcia arranged a long-term lease for the historically and culturally significant building at 301 Washington Avenue. The 1936 structure (the original temple building, immediately to the north, was built in 1929) had been designed by Henry Hohauser and it featured seventy-seven stained-glass windows, a Moorish copper dome, Art Deco chandeliers, a marble bimah and 7,200 square feet of space on three levels in which to house the museum, offices, research area and exhibitions.

Led by famed architect Ira Giller, the museum raised $1.5 million for the renovation, with assistance from the City of Miami Beach, Miami-Dade Cultural Affairs Council, the State of Florida and private and foundation funding.

In 2005, the museum purchased from the synagogue the three contiguous properties including the leased building (301 Washington Avenue), the original synagogue at 311 Washington and the parking lot next door, immediately thereafter beginning major expansion plans. In 2007, after a year-long million-dollar-plus restoration, the museum opened its second major area, which housed the first synagogue on Miami Beach. In 2008, a skylighted café connecting the two buildings was opened and future plans call for a collections and research center to be built over the parking lot.

Visitors to the museum can enjoy the core exhibit, "MOSAIC: Jewish Life in Florida," as well as changing Jewish art and history exhibits, forty of which have been presented to the public through 2008. A number of permanent features—including a timeline of Florida's Jewish history, several films, a museum store and a collections and research center that is used daily—further enhance the museum experience.

The museum is open Tuesdays through Sundays from 10:00 a.m. until 5:00 p.m. and is staffed by a dedicated group of both paid personnel and volunteers, with docents who offer tours through the museum. Suffice to say that the Jewish Museum of Florida is one of the true treasures of the entire state as well as of and for American Jewry.

Unless otherwise credited, all photographs in this chapter are courtesy of the Jewish Museum of Florida.

Above: The stunningly beautiful Jewish Museum of Florida glows like a light of learning, a beacon for students and historians of Florida and Jewish history. *Courtesy Jeff Weisberg.*

Right: From 1993 to 1995, the building at 301 Washington Avenue was completely restored for its opening as the Jewish Museum of Florida.

From 1990 until 1994, the original MOSAIC exhibit went "on the road," traveling to thirteen cities in Florida to bring the story of Florida's Jewish people and their great and incredible contributions to the entire state.

In 1995, the museum opened in the restored former synagogue at 301 Washington Avenue, featuring its core exhibit.

The Bonim exhibit is one of forty temporary exhibits that have been presented by the museum, almost every one of them to major critical acclaim.

In April of 2007, the magnificently restored building that had been the original synagogue at 311 Washington Avenue opened. The exhibit hall is shown here.

The two museum buildings, including the Center Court Café that connects the buildings, were completed in 2008. Further expansion plans call for a collections and research center to be built over the parking lot that the museum owns just north of the 311 Washington Avenue building.

As with the Federation and the Jewish Home, there are innumerable individuals who have contributed to the success of the great project known as the Jewish Museum of Florida. From those who have served as presidents of the museum to and through the incomparable Ira Giller, as well as all who have worked or volunteered there, success is built upon all working together. But, as with the other organizations, it takes a terrific leader to guide all of those caring, interested and devoted people, and in the case of the Jewish Museum that person—the person who will always be identified with the museum—is Marcia Zerivitz. Shown here with husband Elliott, Marcia, like Samuel Gertner, the Cypens and Stanley C. Myers, will remain in our hearts and in our minds as the person to whom the greatest debt of gratitude is owed, and like her illustrious counterparts, the entire community is grateful to those leaders for all they have done to help build one of the greatest and most important Jewish communities in America, if not in the entire world.